Gresham Books Ltd
The Carriage House
Ningwood Manor
Ningwood
Isle of Wight
PO30 4NJ

Text copyright © NRR Oulton 1999
Illustrations copyright © Ian Douglass 1999
First published 1999 by Galore Park Ltd
This edition published by Gresham Books Ltd 2020
Typesetting by Gresham Books Ltd
Printed in the United Kingdom

All rights reserved: no part of this publication may be reproduced, stored in a retrieval system, or transmitted in any form or by any means, electronic, mechanical, photocopying, recording or otherwise, without either the prior written permission of the copyright owner or a licence permitting restricted copying issued by the Copyright Licensing Agency, 5th Floor, Shackleton House, 4 Battlebridge Lane, London, SE1 2HX.

To Branny, Cotta, Labienus and the pin cushions, with grateful thanks.

ISBN 978-0-946095-63-6

Also available in the So You Really Want to Learn Latin series:

Book I Answer Book	ISBN 978-0-946095-66-7
So you really want to learn Latin Book II	ISBN 978-0-946095-64-3
• Book II Answer Book	ISBN 978-0-946095-67-4
So you really want to learn Latin Book III	ISBN 978-0-946095-65-0
• Book III Answer Book	ISBN 978-0-946095-68-1

You can find more resources at
www.soyoureallywanttolearnlatin.co.uk

Contents

PREFACE 1
GUIDE TO PRONUNCIATION 2
    Vowels 2
    Diphthongs 2
    Vowel and syllable length 2
    Consonants 3
    Stress 3
INTRODUCTION 5
CHAPTER I 6
    Verbs 6
    amō: present tense 6
    Verbs like amō 6
    The future tense 8
    The imperfect tense 8
    And, but, not 8
    Vocabulary 1 8
    Principal parts 10
    The perfect tense 10
    English derivations 12
    Revision 12
    Points to remember 12
    Aeneas and the origins of Rome 14
CHAPTER 2 16
    Nouns like mēnsa 16
    The six cases 16
    Subjects and objects 18
    Subjects and objects in Latin 18
    Verbs in the sentence 18
    Subjects 'in the verb' 20
    Nouns in the vocabulary 20
    Vocabulary 2 20
    Translating from Latin: Golden Rules 22
    Revision 22
    Romulus and Remus 24
CHAPTER 3 26
    Using all the cases 26
    Nominative case 26
    Vocative case 26
    Accusative case 26
    Genitive case 26
    Dative case 26
    Ablative case 26
    More on the genitive 28

Coping with all the cases: from Latin	28
New vocabulary	29
Prepositions	30
Vocabulary 3	30
Clauses	32
English derivations: prefixes and suffixes	32
The Foundation of Rome	34
CHAPTER 4	**36**
Verbs of the 2nd conjugation: moneō	36
Principal parts: 2nd conjugation	36
Nouns of the 2nd declension: annus	38
Stems and endings	38
A word of caution	38
Nouns like bellum	40
Working with neuters	40
Dealing with the simple past	42
Vocabulary 4	42
The Sabine women	44
Festivals	45
Revision	45
CHAPTER 5	**46**
Adjectives like bonus	46
Agreement of adjectives	46
puer and magister	48
Adjectives in –er	50
Vocabulary 5	52
Plural nouns	52
Other modern languages	52
The first Roman traitress	54
CHAPTER 6	**56**
Verbs like regō	56
Problems with regō	56
Questions in Latin	58
-ne, nōnne, num: points to note	58
Verbs like audiō	60
Points to note with audiō	60
The historic present	60
Vocabulary 6	62
Verbs with yukky principal parts	62
The kings of Rome (part 1)	64
CHAPTER 7	**66**
Verbs like capiō	66
Breaking up inverted commas: inquit / inquiunt	66
Roman numerals	68
Numerals 11–1000!	68
fīlius, deus, vir	70

- Vocabulary 7 70
- Revision 70
- The kings of Rome (part 2) 72

CHAPTER 8 74
- 3rd declension nouns: rēx and opus 74
- Working with 3rd declension nouns 74
- Common nouns 74
- Agreement of adjectives with 3rd declension nouns 76
- Adjectives and common nouns 76
- Vocabulary 8 76
- Apposition 76
- nōmine = by name 76
- Non-increasing 3rd declension nouns: cīvis and cubīle 78
- Common exceptions 78
- Horatius holds the bridge 80

CHAPTER 9 82
- Linking sentences and clauses 82
- And…not 84
- But…not 84
- nec…nec and et…et 84
- Vocabulary 9 84
- Mucius Scaevola 86
- Revision 87

CHAPTER 10 88
- The verb 'to be' 88
- sum and complements 88
- There is / there are 88
- To be or not to be? 90
- The last two tenses: future perfect and pluperfect 90
- Points to note 90
- Using the principal parts 92
- Vocabulary 10 92
- The escape of Cloelia, 508 B.C 94

SUMMARY OF GRAMMAR 96
- Verbs 96
- Nouns 98
- Cardinal Numerals 99
- Ordinals 99
- Adjectives 100

APPENDIX 101
- More on vowel quantity 101

LATIN – ENGLISH VOCABULARY 102

ENGLISH – LATIN VOCABULARY 107

Acknowledgements

The author would like to thank the following who have all contributed to the production of this book:

Theo Zinn, who taught me Latin and showed me, above all, that if you <u>really</u> want to learn something, you have to learn it properly and whose advice, particularly on vowel quantities, has been invaluable; Stephen Anderson, who read the proofs of the book and pointed out its numerous faults and errors with great tact and infinite patience – the errors that remain are, of course, entirely my own; the girls of Tormead School, who put up with the various revisions of the book and pointed out its faults and misprints on a daily basis; in particular I should like to thank Nikki Lake, who shot through the original version of the whole course in two terms flat and pointed out several glaring errors with an ever cheerful 'It's probably me, but shouldn't there be a verb in this sentence...?'; Roland Smith, for coping with the endless stream of 'last minute changes'; Honor Alleyne, for inspiring me to write the book in the first place, and for allowing me to inflict it on the girls of Tormead without so much as a government health warning; and the countless colleagues who have commented on this and earlier versions of the book and given me their support. I shall not give the traditional acknowledgement to my wife, Claire, because she said she would kill me if I did.

This edition includes a very small number of alterations and corrections to some of the exercises. These are as follows:
Ex. 1.2, Q.4
Ex. 1.3, Q.9
Ex. 3.11, Q.1
Ex. 4.5, Q.1-3
Ex. 6.14, Q.1 and Q.3

PREFACE

This is a no-nonsense Latin text book. No frills, not many pictures, and definitely no word searches. Learning Latin is not the easiest thing you could choose to do. In fact, some of you will find it devilishly difficult. But it *can* be done and you will just have to accept the fact that it involves a good memory and loads of discipline.

In this book, things that have to be learnt are on the left-hand pages; things that have to be done are on the right. As you learn something on the left, you practise it on the right. Simple, isn't it? If you can cope with this lot, Books II and III will take you all the way up to GCSE level and beyond.

It has to be said that you won't be able to tell the time in Latin, or sing a comic song. But you will have bashed up a couple of hundred thousand Gauls with arrows, and prepared a good many tables for the master. What's more, your brain will have done so many mental somersaults and press-ups that you will find anything else you turn to laughably easy by comparison.

N.R.R.O.
April 1999

YouTube video references

P.S. You can now follow the course on YouTube - don't let anyone tell you that Latin is dead! Throughout the book, you will find references to the YouTube videos that accompany this course. References beginning **H** refer to the History videos; references beginning **1.** refer to the videos in the Latin 1 Playlist. The one beginning **LP** refers to the Latin Pronunciation video. All of these can be found on the So you really want to learn Latin YouTube channel at: www.youtube.com/soyoureallywanttolearnlatin

GUIDE TO PRONUNCIATION

Vowels

The main problem with learning to pronounce Latin correctly is the vowels. The Romans, as Asterix is always telling us, were crazy and they pronounced their vowels as follows:

ă (short)	as in cup	ā (long)	as in calf
ĕ (short)	as in set	ē (long)	as in stair
ĭ (short)	as in bit	ī (long)	as in bee
ŏ (short)	as in lot	ō (long)	as in the French *beau*
ŭ (short)	as in put	ū (long)	as in route

In this book, *long* vowels are marked with a macron (ā, ē, ī, ō, ū). If they are *not* marked, they are short. Occasionally a short vowel is marked as short (ă, ĕ, ĭ, ŏ, ŭ) if there is an incorrect tendency to pronounce the vowel long. For example the o in the Latin word egŏ is marked as short because so many people pronounce the word as if it were long.

Just occasionally a vowel may be marked as being both long *and* short. This is where a vowel is known to have been pronounced long in some places but short in others. In this book, for example, you will come across the words quandō̆ and homō̆, the final 'o's of which are sometimes pronounced long, sometimes short. You will also find ubī̆ and ibī̆, the final 'i's of which may be either long or short.

A vowel is regularly pronounced long when followed by ns or nf. This rule even applies to the word in when this is followed by a word starting with s or f.
E.g. **in** agrō but **īn** silvā.

Diphthongs

Where two vowels are pronounced as *one* sound (as in the English *boil*, or *wait*), this is called a **diphthong** and the resulting syllable will always be long. For example the –ae of the word mēnsae is a diphthong. Diphthongs, because they are always long, are not marked with a macron.

The most common diphthongs are:

ae	as in eye	au	as in now

but you may also find:

ei	as in reign	oe	as in boil
ui	as in French *oui*	eu	as in e and u said in one breath!

Vowel and syllable length

You need to learn the quantity of a *vowel* (i.e. whether it is long or short) to ensure that you pronounce the word correctly. But you also need to know the length of the *syllable* that the vowel is in. This is because Latin poetry was based on the subtle combination of long and short syllables.

I don't want to put you off before you even start, but you should know that there is a difference between marking a vowel as long or short and saying that the syllable itself is long or short. A syllable is long:
(a) if it contains a long vowel; or
(b) if it contains a vowel followed by two consonants.
For the purposes of this rule, x and z count as double consonants as does the consonant i (see below) where this comes between two vowels (see Appendix on page 101).

Consonants

- C is always *hard* as in cot, never *soft* as in century.
- R is always rolled.
- S is always 's' as in bus, never 'z' as in busy.
- V is pronounced as a W.
- GN is pronounced NGN, as in hangnail.
- Latin has no letter J. The Romans used i as a consonant instead (thus Iūlius Caesar, pronounced Yulius).
- M, at the end of a word, was nasalised and reduced (i.e. only partially pronounced).

Stress

Just as in English we have a particular way of stressing words, so they did in Latin. We, for example, say potáto (with the stress on the a). When we learn English words, we automatically learn how to stress them. This would have been the same for the Romans, learning Latin words.

The Romans worked out how to stress a word by looking at its penultimate syllable. Syllables, as we have seen, are either long or short. They are long if they contain a long vowel, or if they contain a short vowel followed by two consonants. They are short if they contain a short vowel which is *not* followed by two consonants. Using this information, a Latin word should be stressed as follows:

- The final syllable of a word should never be stressed (e.g. ámō, ámās, ámat, etc.)
- In a word of more than two syllables, if the penultimate syllable is long, stress it (e.g. amātis is stressed amátis; amāvistis* is stressed amāvístis).
- If the penultimate syllable is short, stress the one before it (e.g. regĭtis is stressed régitis).

* Note how the penultimate syllable of amāvistis is long because the i, although short, is followed by two consonants (st).

4

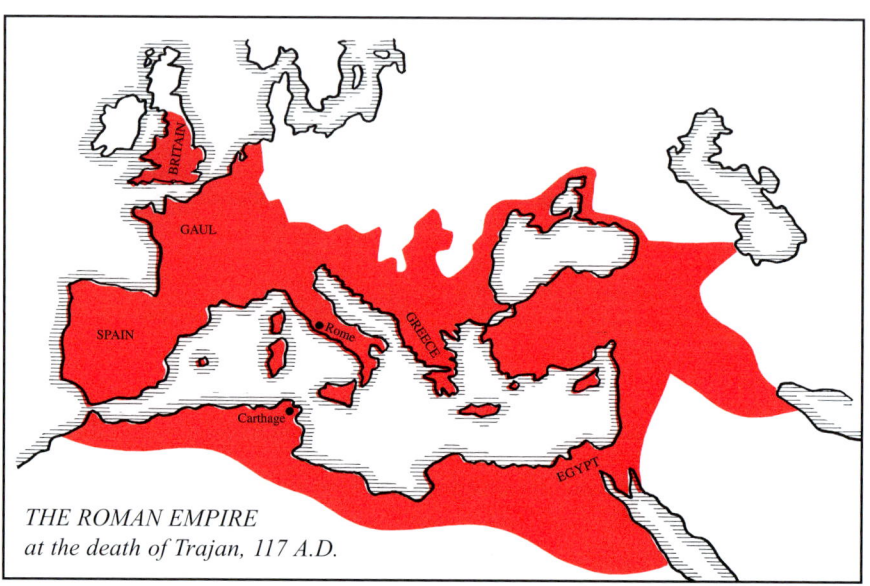

INTRODUCTION

Latin was the language spoken by the ancient Romans. Because the Romans conquered so much of the world, Latin was spoken in several countries and for hundreds of years continued to be spoken and written, even after the Romans had gone. Gradually changes developed in the way Latin was used in each of these countries. In Italy, Latin became Italian; in France it became French; in Spain it became Spanish.

In Britain, Latin did not become the basis of the English language as it did for many of the other European languages. But, with the arrival of the Normans in 1066, much of the old Anglo-Saxon language and customs was augmented by Norman (i.e. French) language and customs. The educated classes, the clergy and the new Norman officials who had come to rule Britain, used Latin, as they did on the continent, as the official written language of government. As a result a huge number of words of Latin origin passed into the English language.

The Romans ruled an empire which extended to most of modern Europe and beyond to Palestine, Egypt and north Africa. Their skill at engineering and construction was unmatched until the 20th century, and their form of administration, considering the size of their empire, was remarkable. But they could also be a cruel, bloodthirsty lot, who enjoyed watching animals being torn to bits in the arena, or gladiators fighting to the death with tridents.

We study Latin today for a number of reasons. It provides an excellent basis for learning language, both our own language and modern languages which are formed from Latin. It provides an excellent form of mental gymnastics, exercising our brains and training them to memorise, analyse and deduce. And of course it allows us to learn more about this remarkable people, to read their literature, enjoy their stories and thus come to appreciate the Romans who ruled the world for so many hundreds of years.

sine quā nōn
A sine quā nōn is something which is essential.
In Latin sine quā nōn = without which not.

CHAPTER I
Verbs: the 1st conjugation

Verbs

Before we can begin in Latin, we need to understand how verbs work. The verb in a sentence tells us *what is happening*, and *who* is doing it. In Latin, verbs have a *stem*, which tells us what is happening, and an *ending*, which tells us who is doing it.

Verbs have three **persons**: 1st, 2nd and 3rd; and two **numbers**: singular and plural. The ending of the verb alters depending on the person and number of the verb. The person and number show us who is doing the verb.

amō: present tense

The **tense** shows us *when* the verb is being done. In Latin there are six tenses. The first of these is the present tense, which tells us what is happening *now*.

The present tense of amō is as follows:

amō = I love, I like		
1st person singular	**am-ō***	I love
2nd person singular	**amā-s**	You (sing.) love
3rd person singular	**ama-t**	He, she or it loves
1st person plural	**amā-mus**	We love
2nd person plural	**amā-tis**	You (pl.) love
3rd person plural	**ama-nt**	They love

* The present stem of amō is amā-. The present tense endings are -ō, -s, -t, -mus, -tis and -nt. In the 1st person singular the stem of verbs like amō contracts from amā- to am-, but it quickly recovers the missing ā and is rarely to be seen without it again.

N.B. the present tense in English can be *love*, *am loving* or *do love*.

Verbs like amō

Verbs are divided into four main groups called **conjugations**. Verbs of the 1st conjugation go like amō. Thus cantō = I sing (present stem cantā-), and aedificō = I build (present stem = aedificā-), go:

cant-ō	I sing		**aedific-ō**	I build
cantā-s	You (sing.) sing		**aedificā-s**	You (sing.) build
canta-t	He, she or it sings		**aedifica-t**	He, she or it builds
cantā-mus	We sing		**aedificā-mus**	We build
cantā-tis	You (pl.) sing		**aedificā-tis**	You (pl.) build
canta-nt	They sing		**aedifica-nt**	They build

So you really want to learn Latin...

Exercise 1.1

Study the information on the left-hand page. Notice how cantō and aedificō, written out in the present tense, use exactly the same endings as amō. All 1st conjugation verbs copy amō in this way. N.B. The hyphen between the stem and the endings is only given on the left-hand page to help you recognise the two parts of the word. You do not need to use hyphens in the exercises that follow. Now write out the present tense of the following verbs, *together with their meanings*:

1. vocō = I call
2. nāvigō = I sail
3. festīnō = I hurry
4. labōrō = I work

Exercise 1.2

Make a note of the seven Latin verbs you have met so far, with their meanings (e.g. aedificō = I build, etc.). Note how the present tense of amō can mean *I love, am loving* or *do love*. Then translate into Latin:

1. I am loving
2. You (sing.) are sailing
3. They are hurrying
4. He does work
5. She is calling
6. You (pl.) like
7. We sing
8. It sails
9. You (pl.) build
10. He is singing

Exercise 1.3

Translate into English. Each Latin word has three possible English translations (e.g. *I love, am loving* or *do love*). Use whichever one you wish.

1. cantat
2. amās
3. nāvigās
4. vocātis
5. aedificant
6. festīnātis
7. festīnās
8. aedificō
9. labōrās
10. vocat

Exercise 1.4

Translate into Latin:

1. We are building
2. They do sing
3. She is hurrying
4. They sail
5. We are working
6. I do love
7. You (pl.) do call
8. He does sail
9. We call
10. You (sing.) are hurrying

Using Latin

N.B.
The letters N.B. stand for notā bene = Note well!

The future tense

So far we have only used the present tense, telling us what is happening *now*. But if we want to know what *will* or *shall* happen in the future, we need to use the future tense, sometimes called the future simple tense. The future tense of amō is set out below. Note how the endings are added to the present stem (amā-) which you met earlier.

amā-**bō**	I shall love / will love
amā-**bis**	You (sing.) will love
amā-**bit**	He, she, it will love
amā-**bimus**	We shall love / will love
amā-**bitis**	You (pl.) will love
amā-**bunt**	They will love

The imperfect tense

The imperfect tense refers to a continuous action in the past. Thus, if we wish to know what *was happening* or *used to happen* in the past, we use the imperfect tense. Again, all we do is add a different set of endings to our old friend the present stem (amā-):

amā-**bam**	I was loving, used to love
amā-**bās**	You (sing.) were loving
amā-**bat**	He, she, it was loving
amā-**bāmus**	We were loving
amā-**bātis**	You (pl.) were loving
amā-**bant**	They were loving

And, but, not

Verbs may be joined by the conjunctions et = and or sed = but. Thus: amat et cantat = He loves and sings. They may be made negative by using the adverb nōn = not, which is always placed *before* the verb, not after it. Thus: nōn amat = He does not love.

Vocabulary 1

Verbs

aedificō	I build	oppugnō	I attack (a city)		
amō	I love, like	parō	I prepare		
cantō	I sing	pugnō	I fight		
exspectō	I wait (for)	rogō	I ask		
festīnō	I hurry	spectō	I watch		
labōrō	I work	superō	I overcome		
nāvigō	I sail	vocō	I call		

Adverb

nōn	not

Conjunctions

et	and
sed	but

So you really want to learn Latin...

Exercise 1. 5
Study the information on the left-hand page about the future tense. Notice how the endings are added to the present stem of the verb. Notice also how the word *shall* should really be used instead of *will* in the 1st person. Now translate into Latin:

1. I shall build
2. They will build
3. You (sing.) will sing
4. It will sail
5. He will hurry
6. We shall hurry
7. You (pl.) will love
8. They will call
9. You (pl.) will work
10. We shall call

Exercise 1. 6
Translate into English. N.B. *not all* of these verbs are in the future tense.

1. festīnābunt
2. labōrātis
3. aedificātis
4. amābitis
5. vocābit
6. labōrant
7. nāvigābis
8. cantābunt
9. cantās
10. aedificābitis

Exercise 1. 7
Study the information on the left-hand page about the imperfect tense. Note the two ways of expressing this tense in English. Then translate into Latin:

1. I was building
2. They were working
3. You (sing.) were sailing
4. He used to build
5. She was singing
6. You (pl.) were hurrying
7. We used to hurry
8. We were calling
9. You (pl.) used to call
10. They were singing

Exercise 1. 8
Study the information on the left-hand page about *and*, *but* and *not*. Then translate the following. Some new verbs are used (from the vocabulary on the left-hand page).

1. rogābant
2. nōn superābat
3. spectābis
4. festīnābātis et parābam
5. nōn vocābātis
6. pugnābant et superābant
7. pugnat sed labōrāmus
8. vocābat et festīnābat
9. pugnābās sed superābam
10. nōn pugnābimus

Using Latin

i.e.
The letters i.e. stand for id est = that is.

Principal parts

Before moving on to the other tenses in Latin we need to explain how principal parts work. All Latin verbs have strange things called **principal parts**. These are the four main parts of the verb, from which all other parts can be formed. The principal parts of amō are as follows:

1	2	3	4
am-ō	amā-re	amāv-ī	amāt-um
I love	To love	I have loved	In order to love

- The *1st principal part* is the 1st person singular of the present tense and gives us the basic meaning of the verb.
- The *2nd principal part* is the **present infinitive**, and is used to find the **present stem** of the verb (by chopping off the -re).
- The *3rd principal part* is the 1st person singular of the perfect tense, and is used to find the **perfect stem** of the verb (by chopping off the -ī).
- The *4th principal part* is the *supine*. This is a very rare part of the verb, but is useful as it gives us (by chopping off the -um) the **supine stem**, used for forming some of the passive tenses of the verb (described later in the course).

N.B. All the verbs which you have met so far go like amō and form their principal parts in exactly the same way as amō does (i.e. -ō, -āre, -āvī, -ātum). Thus nāvigō = I sail has the following principal parts:

nāvigō	nāvigāre	nāvigāvī	nāvigātum
I sail	To sail	I have sailed	In order to sail

The perfect tense

When we wish to describe a state which is the result in the present of an action which has happened in the past we use the perfect tense. This tense is used to refer to a completed action in the past (unlike the imperfect, which refers to *continuous* actions).

E.g. I have lost my dog; he has lost his marbles; etc.

The perfect tense is formed by adding a set of endings to the **perfect stem**. As we saw above, this is found by looking at the verb's 3rd principal part.

amāv-ī	I have loved
amāv-istī	You (sing.) have loved
amāv-it	He, she, it has loved
amāv-imus	We have loved
amāv-istis	You (pl.) have loved
amāv-ērunt	They have loved

So you really want to learn Latin...

Exercise 1. 9
Read the information on the left-hand page about principal parts. Notice how 1st conjugation verbs like amō tend to form their principal parts in the same way (-ō, -āre, -āvī, -ātum). Write out the principal parts and meanings of the following verbs:

1. vocō
2. aedificō
3. cantō
4. exspectō

Exercise 1. 10
Read the information on the left-hand page about the perfect tense. Then translate into Latin:

1. I have sailed
2. You (sing.) have called
3. You (sing.) have built
4. They have worked
5. She has hurried
6. I have built
7. We have not waited
8. He has sailed
9. You (pl.) have worked
10. We have asked

Exercise 1. 11
Translate into English. Remember that the 2nd principal part of a verb ends in -re and is its present infinitive (*to love, to sing*, etc.):

1. nāvigāvimus
2. amāre
3. vocāvit
4. labōrāvērunt
5. festīnāvistis
6. nāvigāvērunt
7. labōrāvī et aedificāvī
8. nōn vocāvī
9. nōn aedificāvistī
10. festīnāre

Exercise 1. 12
You have now learnt how to use four tenses plus the present infinitive in Latin. Taking care over which endings to use, translate the following into Latin:

1. We build
2. To work
3. You (sing.) will hurry
4. We were sailing
5. They were calling
6. You (pl.) will like
7. To fight
8. You (sing.) have called
9. I shall not build
10. She does not work

Using Latin

e.g.
The letters e.g. stand for exemplī grātiā
= for the sake of example.

English derivations

Many English words are derived from Latin ones. It is often possible to work out the meaning of an English word if you recognise the Latin root from which it is derived.

E.g. the English adjective pugnacious comes from the Latin verb pugnō = I fight and describes someone who likes fighting.

In years to come you will probably find yourself droning on about the importance of Latin, how it helps with the meaning and spelling of words, how it ought to be compulsory...

Revision

Well done! You have got through the first chapter and are almost ready for nouns. So this is a good time to revise carefully everything you have learnt about 1st conjugation verbs. Make sure you learn this information by heart. Life will be trickier than a great big tricky thing if you find that you need to keep flicking back to chapter one every time you meet a verb.

amō, amāre, amāvī, amātum = I love, like

Present Tense		Imperfect Tense	
am-ō	I love	amā-bam	I was loving, used to love
amā-s	You love	amā-bās	etc
ama-t	He, she, it loves	amā-bat	
amā-mus	We love	amā-bāmus	
amā-tis	You love	amā-bātis	
ama-nt	They love	amā-bant	

Future Tense		Perfect Tense	
amā-bō	I shall / will love	amāv-ī	I have loved
amā-bis	etc.	amāv-istī	etc.
amā-bit		amāv-it	
amā-bimus		amāv-imus	
amā-bitis		amāv-istis	
amā-bunt		amāv-ērunt	

Points to remember

Make sure that you have learnt by heart:
1. amō in the four tenses you have met so far
2. The principal parts of amō
3. The various ways of translating the four tenses you have learnt
4. The meanings of the words in Vocabulary 1
5. nōn = 'not' and comes *before* the verb, not after (e.g. nōn amat)

So you really want to learn Latin...

Exercise 1. 13
Read the information on the left-hand page about English derivations. From which Latin words do the following English ones derive? Translate the Latin word and explain the meaning of the English one.
E.g. Pugnacious = keen on fighting; from pugnō = I fight.

1. Laboratory
2. Navigate
3. Vocation
4. Expect

Exercise 1. 14
Read through the revision section on the left-hand page and then translate into Latin:

1. He builds
2. They were fighting
3. We will sing
4. You (pl.) have sailed
5. They were not watching
6. He does not fight
7. You (sing.) used to like
8. We shall not watch
9. She has sailed
10. I was waiting

Exercise 1. 15
Translate into English:

1. aedificant
2. festīnāre
3. nōn pugnābāmus
4. nāvigābitis
5. cantābam sed labōrābās
6. nāvigābātis
7. pugnāvit et superāvit
8. spectātis
9. aedificābis
10. nāvigāvistis

Exercise 1. 16
Give the principal parts and meanings of:

1. labōrō
2. parō
3. cantō
4. aedificō

Exercise 1. 17
Translate into English, being careful to use the correct tense:

1. amāvērunt
2. amābit
3. amātis
4. amābat
5. amābimus
6. amāvit
7. amābās
8. amāvistis

Using Latin

circā
c. or circā (= around) is often used with dates to show that they are approximate. E.g. He died c.1815.

Aeneas and the origins of Rome

So who were these Romans, anyway? According to legend Rome was founded by Romulus in 753 B.C. However the story starts long before that, dating back to the time of the Trojan War. The ancient city of Troy was captured and destroyed in around 1250 B.C. by a Greek army led by Agamemnon, king of Mycenae. All of its inhabitants were either killed or led into slavery; all, that is, except for a brave band of men led by the Trojan prince, Aeneas. This man, the son of the goddess Venus, was ordered to set out from the burning city, carrying the household gods, with his aged father Anchises on his back and holding his young son Ascanius (or Iulus) by the hand. After many adventures and a long, dangerous journey, Aeneas eventually arrived in Italy where he fought with a local prince, Turnus, for the hand of Lavinia, daughter of King Latinus. After defeating Turnus, Aeneas married the girl and built a new city which he named Lavinium. These stories are told in Virgil's great epic poem the Aeneid.

Aeneas's son, Ascanius, soon left Lavinium and went off to found his own city. It was in this city, Alba Longa, many generations later, that the true founder of Rome, Romulus, was born.

So you really want to learn Latin...

Exercise 1. 18

Read the story of Aeneas and the origins of Rome on the left-hand page. Write the heading 'Aeneas and the origins of Rome'. Then answer the following questions in complete sentences.

1. According to legend, who founded Rome, and in which year?
2. The story of Rome's foundation dates back to the time of which legendary war?
3. Who was the leader of the Greek army and in which year, approximately, did he capture Troy?
4. What happened to most of the inhabitants of Troy?
5. Who was Aeneas?
6. Why did Aeneas leave Troy after it had been captured?
7. Which objects was he ordered to take with him?
8. Which people did he take with him?
9. After his long, dangerous journey, in which country did Aeneas eventually arrive?
10. With whom did he fight when he got there?
11. Over which girl did Aeneas fight, and whose daughter was she?
12. What was the name of the city Aeneas built?
13. What did Ascanius do once his father had built the new city?
14. Who was born many generations later in Ascanius's new city?

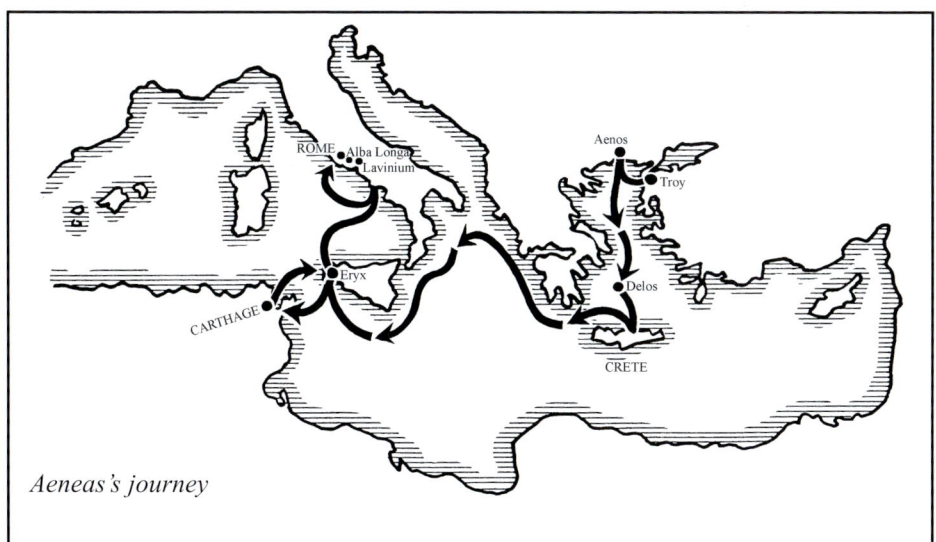

Aeneas's journey

Using Latin

versus
versus = turned against. If Chelsea play versus Liverpool, they play *against* them.

CHAPTER 2

Nouns of the 1st declension; subjects and objects

Nouns like mēnsa

In the same way that verbs in Latin have endings to show *who* is doing the verb, and *when*, nouns in Latin have endings to show *what part* the noun is playing in the sentence.

As with verbs, nouns are divided up into groups, and these are called **declensions**. Nouns of the 1st declension decline like mēnsa:

Singular

Nominative	mēns-a	Table (subject)
Vocative	mēns-a	O table! (addressing)
Accusative	mēns-am	Table (object)
Genitive	mēns-ae	Of a table
Dative	mēns-ae	To or for a table
Ablative	mēns-ā	By, with or from a table

Plural

Nominative	mēns-ae	Tables (subject)
Vocative	mēns-ae	O tables! (addressing)
Accusative	mēns-ās	Tables (object)
Genitive	mēns-ārum	Of the tables
Dative	mēns-īs	To or for the tables
Ablative	mēns-īs	By, with or from the tables

The six cases

Nouns in Latin can be put into one of six **cases** (nominative, vocative, accusative, genitive, dative or ablative) and one of two **numbers** (singular or plural).

The **Nominative** case is used to show that the noun is the **subject** of the sentence, i.e. that the noun is the person or thing *doing the verb*.

The **Vocative** case is used for **addressing** the noun. Not so common with tables, I hear you say, but if the noun were a name such as Flavia we would put her into the vocative case when addressing her. 'O Flavia' we would say. 'O Flavia, how nice to see you!'

The **Accusative** case is used to show that the noun is the **object**, i.e., the person or thing *to which the verb is being done*.

The **Genitive** case is used for *of*.

The **Dative** case is used for *to* or *for*.

The **Ablative** case is used for *by*, *with* or *from*. Note that the ablative singular ends in a long ā, which makes it sound different from the nominative and vocative singular.

N.B. Latin has no definite or indefinite article. Thus mēnsa = 'table' or 'the table' or 'a table' – the choice is yours.

So you really want to learn Latin...

Exercise 2.1

Study the information on the left-hand page about mēnsa. Notice how the ending of a Latin noun changes to reflect its meaning. All nouns of the 1st declension go like mēnsa. We could thus write out the 1st declension nouns puella = a girl, and agricola = a farmer, as follows:

Nominative	puell-a	agricol-a
Vocative	puell-a	agricol-a
Accusative	puell-am	agricol-am
Genitive	puell-ae	agricol-ae
Dative	puell-ae	agricol-ae
Ablative	puell-ā	agricol-ā
Nominative	puell-ae	agricol-ae
Vocative	puell-ae	agricol-ae
Accusative	puell-ās	agricol-ās
Genitive	puell-ārum	agricol-ārum
Dative	puell-īs	agricol-īs
Ablative	puell-īs	agricol-īs

This is called writing out a noun in full. Write out the following nouns in full:

1. incola = inhabitant
2. fābula = story
3. nauta = sailor
4. rēgīna = queen

Exercise 2.2

Study the information on the left-hand page about the different meanings for each of the six cases. Then give the Latin for:

1. Of the farmer
2. To the sailor
3. Of a story
4. By a story
5. O farmers!
6. The farmers (subject)
7. The farmer (object)
8. For the sailors
9. O sailor!
10. Of the farmers

Using Latin

E.R.
The letters E.R. stand for Elizabetha Rēgīna = Queen Elizabeth.

Subjects and objects

The most important distinction which you must learn to make when dealing with nouns is that between subject and object.

1. The subject of a sentence is the person or thing *doing the verb*. E.g. *The girl loves the farmer*. In this romantic example, *the girl* is the subject because she is doing the loving.
2. The object (or *direct* object, as it should really be called), is the person or thing *having the verb done to him* (or *her* or *it*). Thus in our example above, *the farmer* is the object because he is the one getting loved!

We can thus analyse a simple English sentence using the initial **S** for subject, **V** for verb and **O** for object as follows:

S	V	O
The girl	loves	the farmer.

Subjects and objects in Latin

English makes it obvious who the subject is and who the object is by means of the **word order**. Thus we can tell at once the difference between *the girl loves the farmer* (where *the girl* is the subject) and *the farmer loves the girl* (where *the farmer* is the subject).

But in Latin this distinction is made, not by means of word order, but by means of **endings**. The nominative case ending shows that a noun is the subject and the accusative case ending shows that it is the object.
Thus:

S	V	O		S	O	V
The girl	loves	the farmer.	=	puella	agricolam	amat.
		or		O	S	V
				agricolam	puella	amat.
		or		V	O	S
				amat	agricolam	puella.

Verbs in the sentence

The verb in Latin very often, but not always, comes at the end of the sentence.
E.g. The girl loves the farmer. = puella agricolam amat.
E.g. The farmers love the girl. = agricolae puellam amant.

But notice, too, how the *verb ending* changes to reflect who is doing the verb. In the first example the subject was *the girl*, and so the verb ending was 3rd person singular (for *she*). But in the second example the subject was *the farmers*, so the verb ending was 3rd person plural (for *they*).

No wonder they say Latin is good for training the mind!

So you really want to learn Latin...

Exercise 2. 3
Study the information on the left-hand page about subjects and objects. Notice how sentences can be analysed by putting S, V and O over the words. Analyse the following sentences by writing S, V and O over the words.

1. The farmer loves the girl.
2. The girls love the queen.
3. The sailors love the girls.
4. The girls love stories.
5. The sailors will overcome the farmers.
6. The farmers will overcome the sailors.

Exercise 2. 4
Read the information on the left-hand page about subjects and objects in Latin and verbs in the sentence. Then look carefully at your analysis of the sentences above. Now translate them into Latin. Remember the following rules:

- The subject must be in the nominative case: -a (singular) or -ae (plural)
- The object must be in the accusative case: -am (singular) or -ās (plural)
- The verb should normally be at the end, with the correct ending
- Nouns use *noun* endings (like mēnsa)
- Verbs use *verb* endings (like amō)

Exercise 2. 5
Here are some more nouns of the 1st declension:

patria = fatherland, country
aqua = water
via = road, street, way
sagitta = arrow
fēmina = woman
victōria = victory

Using these and the nouns you have already met, translate the following into Latin. N.B. a sentence need not necessarily have a direct object. E.g. *The girl was working* has a subject (*the girl*) and a verb (*was working*) but no object.

1. The sailors love the fatherland.
2. The farmer was not working.
3. The women prepare the tables.
4. The sailors were not fighting.
5. The farmers have prepared a way.
6. The woman will not hurry.
7. The sailors love water.
8. The girl was singing.
9. The woman was calling the girls.
10. The women were singing.

Using Latin

viā
viā = by way. Going to Scotland *via* Carlisle means by way of Carlisle.

Subjects 'in the verb'

The subject of a sentence is sometimes a noun (e.g. the sailors) and sometimes a pronoun (e.g. we). When the subject is a noun, we put that noun into the nominative case in Latin. When it is a pronoun, we say that the subject is 'in the verb', because the pronoun does not normally appear as a separate word (as it does in English), but simply appears as the ending on the verb.

If we wish to analyse the Latin for a sentence in which the subject is 'in the verb', there will be no noun to write S over, so we write V+S over the verb to show that that is where the subject is hiding.

S	V	O		S	O	V
The girl	loves	the farmer.	=	puella	agricolam	amat.

S	V	O		O	V+S	
She	loves	the farmer.	=	agricolam	amat.	

N.B. When a sentence has its subject 'in the verb', the first word we write in Latin will normally be the object, which we must remember to put in the accusative case.

Nouns in the vocabulary

When we list nouns in the vocabulary, we give three pieces of information: the genitive singular ending, the gender and the meaning. All three must be learnt.

The genitive singular ending for nouns of the 1st declension is -ae, and so all 1st declension nouns will appear in the vocabulary with the letters -ae after them, e.g. fāma, -ae. Alternatively, the genitive singular may sometimes be written in full, e.g. fāma, fāmae.

The gender of a noun may be masculine (m.), feminine (f.), common (c.) or neuter (n.). *Common* means that the noun can be either masculine or feminine. Neuter is the Latin for neither, and means simply that the noun is neither masculine nor feminine (rather like the English *it*). We will meet some neuter nouns in Chapter 4.

Vocabulary 2

agricola, -ae, m.	farmer	patria, -ae, f.	country, fatherland
aqua, -ae, f.	water	puella, -ae, f.	girl
fābula, -ae, f.	story	pugna, -ae, f.	battle
fāma, -ae, f.	fame, glory	Rōma, -ae, f.	Rome
fēmina, -ae, f.	woman	sagitta, -ae, f.	arrow
Graecia, -ae, f.	Greece	sapientia, -ae, f.	wisdom
incola, -ae, c.	inhabitant	terra, -ae, f.	land, ground
īnsula, -ae, f.	island	Troia, -ae, f.	Troy
mēnsa, -ae, f.	table	via, -ae, f.	road, street, way
nauta, -ae, m.	sailor	victōria, -ae, f.	victory

So you really want to learn Latin...

Exercise 2. 6

Read the information on the left-hand page about subjects 'in the verb'. Then translate into Latin:

1. We love the stories.
2. The sailor loves stories.
3. They overcome the country.
4. The woman loves water.
5. He has overcome the sailor.
6. They will call the farmer.
7. I will not prepare the table.
8. They prepare the tables.
9. You (pl.) have built a road.
10. She has called the girl.

Exercise 2. 7

Study the information on the left-hand page about nouns in the vocabulary. Note down and learn all the words in Vocabulary 2. Then, to revise the meanings of all the cases, give the Latin for:

1. Of the sailor
2. The inhabitants (object)
3. The islands (subject)
4. O woman!
5. O girls!
6. Wisdom (object)
7. Of the way
8. Of the battles
9. The story (subject)
10. Of fame

Exercise 2. 8

Translate into Latin. Note that proper names (such as Greece, Rome and Troy) are nouns and must be put into the correct case.

1. The women love wisdom.
2. The inhabitants have overcome the sailors.
3. The sailors will not attack Rome.
4. The girls are working.
5. The farmers have prepared the arrows.

Exercise 2. 9

From which Latin words are the following English ones derived? Translate the Latin word and explain the meaning of the English one. E.g. *nautical* describes matters to do with sailing; from nauta = sailor.

1. Feminine
2. Aquatic
3. Fable
4. Laborious
5. Navigate

Using Latin

terra firma
'It's nice to be back on terra firma.'
terra firma = firm ground.

Translating from Latin: Golden Rules

Once you know what you are doing, translating into Latin is very simple. You put the subject in the nominative case, the object in the accusative case, and the verb at the end with the correct ending. Translating *out of* Latin can be a touch tricky at first, but it isn't really any harder. If you follow a few golden rules you should be fine:

Always look at the verb first.

The verb tells us what is happening, and who is doing it. Look at the ending of the verb to see which person it is (I, you, he, etc.) and which tense (present, future, etc.). The verb is often *but not always* at the end of the sentence.

Look for a noun in the nominative case.

Unless the subject is 'in the verb' there will be a noun in the nominative case. If the verb is singular (he, she or it), this noun will be nominative singular. If the verb is plural (they) the noun will be nominative plural (or two or more nouns in the nominative joined by *and*).

Look for a noun in the accusative case.

The object, if there is one, will be in the accusative case. As a general rule you should **never translate an accusative case before the verb**. If you do, you will probably have muddled your subject with your object, a crime for which in the good old days people would be shot!

It will help if you analyse the sentence by writing V over the verb, S over the subject, and O over the object. Remember, if the subject is 'in the verb', write V+S over the verb. Note that it is the *endings*, not the word order, which show whether a noun is the subject or object.

	S	O	V
e.g.	puell**a**	agricol**am**	ama**t**.
	O	S	V
and	agricol**am**	puell**a**	ama**t**.

both mean *The girl loves the farmer*.

Revision

You should now know by heart:

- amō in four tenses + their meanings
- mēnsa in the singular and plural
- The names and meanings of the six cases
- The words in Vocabularies 1 + 2

So you really want to learn Latin...

Exercise 2. 10

Read the information on the left-hand page about translating from Latin. Look carefully at the endings of the words, highlighted in bold. Analyse each sentence with the letters S, V and O. Do NOT assume that the first word will be the subject, as it usually is in English. Then translate into English.

1. agricol**a** puell**am** ama**t**.
2. agricol**a** naut**ās** superāv**it**.
3. puell**am** fēmin**a** amā**bat**.
4. naut**a** agricol**am** superā**bit**.
5. agricol**am** amā**bant** puell**ae**.
6. fēmin**a** aqu**am** nōn parā**bat**.
7. vi**am** agricol**ae** parāv**ērunt**.
8. naut**a** sagitt**ās** parāv**it**.
9. naut**ae** īnsul**am** amā**bant**.
10. fām**am** ama**nt** incol**ae**.

Exercise 2. 11

Analyse and translate the following sentences. Again, remember that it is the endings that are important, not the word order. This time, some of the subjects are 'in the verb', so be very careful not to translate an accusative case before the verb.

1. incol**ae** Rōm**am** oppugna**nt**.
2. agricol**a** terr**am** parāv**it**.
3. Graeci**am** nōn amā**mus**.
4. puell**ae** mēns**am** parāv**ērunt**.
5. sagitt**ās** nōn parāv**istis**.
6. incol**ās** nōn superā**bimus**.
7. vi**am** parāv**it**.
8. patri**am** nōn amā**s**.
9. agricol**ae** fēmin**am** supera**nt**.
10. Troi**am** fēmin**ae** amā**bant**.

Exercise 2. 12

Look at the revision list on the left-hand page. Then, without looking up, translate the following, paying attention to whether the final a is long (ā) or short:

1. agricolam
2. fēminās
3. nauta
4. fāma
5. aquā
6. pugna
7. īnsulārum
8. incolārum
9. sagittīs
10. sapientiā

Exercise 2. 13

Revision: Without looking up, translate the following:

1. nāvigāre
2. aedificābis
3. sed
4. parant
5. nōn pugnābō
6. labōrāvērunt
7. cantābātis
8. superāvistis
9. festīnāvī
10. amābat

R.I.P.
R.I.P. stands for requiēscat in pāce
= May he/she rest in peace.

Romulus and Remus

Aeneas' son Ascanius left Lavinium to build his own city, Alba Longa. Many generations later the king of Alba Longa, Proca, died leaving two sons, Numitor and Amulius. The younger son, Amulius, seized the throne from Numitor and locked up his brother's daughter, Rhea Silvia, forcing her to become a Vestal Virgin. Vestal Virgins were not allowed to marry.

According to the legend, the god Mars took pity on Rhea Silvia and 'visited' her. Nine months later twin boys, Romulus and Remus, were born, but the babies were immediately discovered and thrown into the River Tiber.

However, it so happened that the river was flooded at the time and when the flood subsided, Romulus and Remus were washed up on the river bank where they were found by a she-wolf. A few days later the boys were found in the she-wolf's cave by a shepherd called Faustulus, who brought the boys up as his own and trained them to be shepherds.

Some years later, as in all good stories, Romulus and Remus were recognised by their old grandfather Numitor. This was because the twins became involved in a dispute between shepherds working for King Amulius and those working for their grandfather, Numitor. Some of Numitor's men dragged Remus before Numitor, accusing him of having stolen some sheep. Numitor thought he recognised the boy, and when Romulus arrived to rescue his brother, and Numitor saw the twins together, he knew that these were his long lost grandsons. He told the twins the story of their birth, and how he himself had been dispossessed by his wicked younger brother. Romulus and Remus were outraged and together they drove Amulius from the kingdom and restored Numitor to the throne.

So you really want to learn Latin...

Exercise 2.14

Read the information on the left-hand page about Romulus and Remus. Then answer the following questions in complete sentences:

1. Who was Ascanius?
2. Which city did he leave when he set off to build his own?
3. What was the name of the city he built?
4. Who should have been king after the death of Proca?
5. Who did become king, though?
6. What did he do to Rhea Silvia?
7. Why do you think he did this?
8. According to the legend, who was the father of Romulus and Remus?
9. What happened to the babies when their birth was discovered?
10. Why were the babies washed up on the river bank?
11. What sort of animal found them there?
12. Who rescued them from the cave?
13. How did Romulus and Remus come to be recognised by their grandfather?
14. What happened to Amulius?
15. Which other stories you know does this one remind you of?

Using Latin

in memoriam
in memoriam is often seen on tombstones, and may be translated 'in memory' (of).

CHAPTER 3
Using all the cases; prepositions; clauses

Using all the cases

So far you have learnt to write out 1st declension nouns in full, and to write and translate sentences involving subjects (in the nominative case) and objects (in the accusative case). So what about all those other cases? The time has come to start addressing those tables ('O table, how nice to see you!') and to start using the 'of's, 'to's, 'for's etc. which we have largely avoided up to now.

Nominative case

Used for the subject.
E.g. *The girl* loves the farmer. = puell**a** agricolam amat.

Vocative case

When addressing a noun, put the noun you are addressing into the vocative case.
E.g. *O sailors*, you love the island. = naut**ae**, īnsulam amātis.

Accusative case

Used for the object.
E.g. He loves *the girl*. = puell**am** amat.

Genitive case

The genitive case is the possessive case. In English we either use the word *of* or else we use an apostrophe. In Latin, the 'possessor' (i.e. the noun doing the possessing) is put into the genitive case and may come *before* or *after* the other noun.
E.g. The table *of the farmers* = mēnsa agricol**ārum** (OR agricol**ārum** mēnsa).
E.g. *The farmer's* table = mēnsa agricol**ae** (OR agricol**ae** mēnsa).

Dative case

The dative case is used for the *indirect object* and is generally translated with *to* or *for*.
E.g. The farmer sings *to the girls*. = agricola puell**īs** cantat.

Ablative case

The ablative case is used for the instrument *by means of* which we do something. It is often translated by the words *by* or *with*, but only when these mean *by means of*.
E.g. They overcome the inhabitants *by means of wisdom*. = incolās sapienti**ā** superant.
E.g. The farmer overcomes the sailor *with arrows*. = agricola nautam sagitt**īs** superat.

So you really want to learn Latin...

Exercise 3. 1

Study the information on the left-hand page about the use of all the cases. Before attempting to translate into Latin, it is a good idea to analyse each sentence, working out which cases you will need. S, V and O will appear as normal, but the extra cases can be added as follows:

S	V	O	Gen.
The farmer	loves	the land	of the inhabitants.

S	V	O	Abl.
The sailor	overcomes	the farmer	with an arrow.

Once you have analysed a sentence like this, it is practically impossible to translate it into Latin incorrectly. The only thing to watch out for is whether the nouns are singular or plural. Now, analyse the following sentences and then translate into Latin:

1. The girls prepare the table of the farmer.
2. The inhabitants love the fame of Troy.
3. We do not attack Rome with arrows.
4. They will prepare a road for the inhabitants.
5. He has prepared the table for the woman.
6. O girls, the farmers are singing to the women.
7. The arrows of the inhabitants overcome the sailors.
8. They were preparing the tables for the women.
9. O farmers, you will not overcome the country with arrows.
10. O sailors, you have not overcome the inhabitants.

Exercise 3. 2

The more complicated a sentence, the more cases will be involved. Some cases will occur more than once in a sentence. There is no need to panic; just put each noun into Latin in the order it comes in English, remembering to put the verb at the end.

1. The inhabitants of Rome love the glory of Greece.
2. The sailors will overcome the inhabitants of the country with arrows.
3. O farmer, the inhabitants of the country have overcome Greece.
4. He was building a road for the inhabitants of the country.
5. The girls are preparing the table for the sailor.

Using Latin

a.m.
The letters a.m. stand for ante merīdiem = before midday.

More on the genitive

Care needs to be taken with the apostrophe in English. Remember that, with most nouns, if the apostrophe comes before the s (e.g. *farmer's*), the possessor is singular; if it comes after the 's' (e.g. *farmers'*) it is plural. If in any doubt, take out the apostrophe and put in the word 'of.' E.g. *the farmer's* table = the table *of the farmer*.

Extra care needs to be taken with English nouns which don't form their plural by adding 's'.
E.g. *the woman's* table = the table *of the woman* (singular);
the women's table = the table *of the women* (plural).

Coping with all the cases: from Latin

We have already seen that some cases in Latin use the same endings. Thus -ae can be genitive singular, dative singular, nominative plural or vocative plural. When we translate longer sentences this can become a problem and we need to get the old brain cells ticking.

For example, study the following sentence:

> incolae   terrae   viam   agricolae   aedificant.

The ending -ae occurs three times in this sentence, so how can we tell which case each one is supposed to be?

The answer is: common sense. If we follow our Golden Rules of translating from Latin we will work out that the verb is aedificant and that the subject could be either incolae, terrae or agricolae. It would make no sense for terrae to be the subject (the lands are building? – I think not!); so our subject is either incolae or agricolae. If we have no other information about the story, we are free to choose which of these is more likely to be the subject. We have chosen incolae, but it would not be wrong to go for agricolae. Our analysis thus looks like this:

> S   O   V
> incolae   terrae   viam   agricolae   aedificant.

At this stage we know the subject, verb and object of the sentence: the inhabitants build the road. So what do we do with terrae and agricolae? As I said, common sense now takes over. They can't be nominative, because we already have our subject, but both words could be genitive singular, dative singular or vocative plural. Vocatives only crop up when people are addressing each other, so we are left with:

> The inhabitants of/to/for the land build the road of/to/for the farmer.

From this we select the most likely meaning (*The inhabitants of the land build the road for the farmer.*) but there may be more than one possible answer. If so, select the one which *you* feel is most likely.

So you really want to learn Latin...

Exercise 3. 3

Study what it says on the left-hand page about the genitive and about coping with all the cases when translating from Latin. Notice how confusions over the endings can be minimised if you follow the rules of translating, finding the verb first, then the subject, then the object. Analyse and translate:

1. puella fābulam fēminīs nārrābat.
2. agricolae viam incolīs aedificābant.
3. incolae Rōmae fāmam Troiae amābant.
4. nautae, agricolās superāvistis!
5. incolae aquam agricolīs parābant.
6. nautae incolam sagittīs superāvērunt.
7. agricolae, viās et terram incolīs parābitis.
8. fābulās Troiae et fāmam Graeciae nōn amant.

New vocabulary

Up until now, every word you have needed has been on the page you are working on, or on a previous page (in which case you should have learnt it!). From now on you may come across words in the exercises which you have not been given. These will normally be in the vocabulary for the chapter, but you may find it easier to look them up at the back.

Exercise 3. 4

Analyse and translate the following:

1. puella fābulās agricolae amābat.
2. agricola fābulam nōn amābat.
3. mēnsam agricolīs fēmina parāvit.
4. puella sagittās agricolīs parābat.
5. agricolae, fēminās sagittīs nōn superābitis.
6. puellae, agricolae fēminās nōn superābunt.
7. incolae Troiae incolās Ītaliae superāvērunt.
8. nautae incolās Ītaliae superāvērunt.

Exercise 3. 5

Translate the following, giving alternative meanings where appropriate:

1. agricolae
2. sapientiā
3. puellīs
4. terrārum
5. aquā
6. fābulārum
7. sagittīs
8. pugnae

Using Latin

p.m.
The letters p.m. stand for post merīdiem = after midday.

Prepositions

Prepositions are words placed before a noun (*pre-positioned*) which give information about that noun. E.g. *under* the table, *on* the table, *around* the table.

In Latin the preposition *governs* (i.e. is followed by) a particular case, either the accusative or the ablative. Some prepositions govern the accusative, some govern the ablative. When you learn the preposition, you have to learn which case it governs.

Here are two Latin prepositions:
ad + accusative = towards;   sub + ablative = under.

Using these two prepositions, we can write:
towards the table = ad mēnsam.
under the tables = sub mēnsīs.

Particular care needs to be taken with the Latin preposition *in*. When it is followed by the accusative it means *into* or *on to*, but when it is followed by the ablative it means *in* or *on*.
E.g. in mēnsam means *on to* the table.
E.g. in mēnsā means *on* the table.

Vocabulary 3

Verbs

ambulō, -āre, -āvī, -ātum	I walk	inter + acc.	among
habitō, -āre, -āvī, -ātum	I live, inhabit	per + acc.	through, along
nārrō, -āre, -āvī, -ātum	I tell	post + acc.	after
portō, -āre, -āvī, -ātum	I carry	prope + acc.	near
vulnerō, -āre, -āvī, -ātum	I wound	**Prepositions + abl.**	
Prepositions + acc.		ā / ab [2] + abl.	by, from
		cum + abl.	with [3]
ad + acc.	towards, to [1]	dē + abl.	down from, concerning
ante + acc.	before	ē, ex [4] + abl.	out of
circum + acc.	around	in + abl.	in, on
contrā + acc.	against	sine + abl.	without
in + acc.	into, on to	sub + abl.	under

1. ad = to, in the sense of *towards* (e.g. he sails to the island, i.e. *towards* the island). This should not be confused with the normal use of the dative case (meaning *to*).
2. The preposition ā becomes ab if the next word begins with a vowel or h.
E.g. ā Graeciā, but ab Ītaliā.
3. The preposition cum = with, in the sense of *together with* (e.g. he walks with the woman, i.e. *together with* the woman). This should not be confused with the normal use of the ablative for *with* meaning *by means of* (e.g. he killed the farmer *with* an arrow, i.e. *by means of* an arrow).
4. The preposition ē becomes ex before a vowel or h.
E.g. ē Graeciā but ex Ītaliā.

So you really want to learn Latin...

Exercise 3. 6
Examine the information on the left-hand page about prepositions. Translate into Latin, using the prepositions from Vocabulary 3.

1. Towards the island
2. Through the streets
3. Into the water
4. Against the inhabitants
5. In the water
6. With the women
7. Near the table
8. Concerning Troy
9. Out of the country
10. After the story

Exercise 3. 7
Translate into English:

1. in viā
2. contrā agricolās
3. in viam
4. ā patriā
5. cum agricolā
6. in pugnam
7. dē mēnsā
8. per viās
9. sub aquā
10. circum Rōmam

Exercise 3. 8
When translating sentences containing prepositions, it is a good idea when analysing to bracket prepositions together with the nouns they govern, as in the first few shown below. A sentence may contain more than one preposition. Translate into English:

1. Aenēās [ā patriā] nāvigāvit.
2. [ad Ītaliam] festīnābat.
3. Aenēās [cum incolīs] Ītaliae pugnat.
4. agricolae Ītaliae circum nautās ambulābant.
5. ad aquam festīnābant.
6. nautae cum agricolīs pugnābant.
7. per viās patriae ambulābant.
8. prope aquam mēnsās parāvērunt.
9. aquam ad mēnsam portābant.
10. fābulās incolīs nārrābant.

Using Latin

sub aquā
sub aquā = under water.

Clauses

A clause is a grammatical unit that contains a verb. Most of the sentences you have translated so far have been single clauses. Life becomes a touch more complicated when a sentence contains more than one clause (and thus more than one verb).

E.g. He **prepares** an arrow and **hurries** towards the farmer.

As you can see, the two clauses are joined together by a conjunction (and). Once you realise that clauses may be joined together like this, there is nothing to panic about. You simply treat each clause separately, with its own subject, verb, object, etc., placing the verbs *at the end of their own little clause*.

E.g. sagittam **parat** et ad agricolam **festīnat**.

Similarly, if you meet a sentence containing more than one clause in Latin, you simply take the first clause first, and then move on to the next. Sentences like this will be easy to spot because there will be more than one verb, with the first clause being linked to the second by a conjunction (e.g. et or sed).

```
         S      prep. + acc.        V        +     O        V+S
e.g. nautae   [ad īnsulam]    nāvigābunt   et  incolas   superabunt. =
```

The sailors will sail to the island and they will overcome the inhabitants.

English derivations: prefixes and suffixes

A *prefix* is a bit added on to the beginning of a word to alter its meaning, e.g. *pre-* or *pro-*. English prefixes are very often derived directly from Latin prepositions. If you know the meaning of the preposition, this will help you with the meaning of the English word. Here are some common English prefixes:

    ab = from   ad = to   circum = around   contra = against

As you can see, these are simply Latin prepositions. If you know what navigation means, therefore, you can work out what *circum*navigation means.

A *suffix* is a bit added on to the end of a word, e.g. -ion. English words are very often derived from the 4th principal part of a Latin verb, by changing the Latin ending -um to the English suffix -ion.
e.g.   nāvigō, nāvigāre, nāvigāvī, nāvigātum
       nāvigāt-um gives navigat-ion.

If you don't know the meaning of an English word, it is often worth working out whether it comes from a Latin verb to see if this will help. If it has the suffix -ion, for example, you can pretty well guarantee that it comes from Latin. Thus, if you were not quite sure what *vocation* meant, the fact that vocō = I call should help you to work out that a vocation is a *calling*.

So you really want to learn Latin...

Exercise 3. 9
Study the information on the left-hand page about clauses. Translate the following into Latin by dividing the sentences into clauses and putting the verbs *at the end of their own clause*.
1. The farmer was working near the table and he was watching the girl.
2. The girl was carrying water and was preparing the table for the women.
3. A sailor was carrying an arrow and was hurrying towards the girl.
4. He has overcome the inhabitants but has wounded the girl with an arrow.
5. The women were hurrying along the street and watching the battle.

Exercise 3. 10
Translate the following into English. Make sure that, in each sentence, you deal with the first clause first, before moving on to the second one.
1. agricolae terram parābant et viam aedificābant.
2. incolae agricolās amābant et fābulās nārrābant.
3. fēminae nōn labōrant sed fābulās agricolīs nārrant.
4. puellae fābulās nōn nārrābant sed agricolās spectābant.
5. agricolae nōn labōrābant sed in aquam festīnābant.

Exercise 3. 11
Study the information on the left-hand page about English derivations. From which Latin words do the following derive (don't forget prefixes!)? Explain the meaning of the English words and translate the Latin ones into English. E.g. navigate means to steer a boat, from nāvigō = I sail.
1. Insulated
2. Fame
3. Inhabit
4. Fabulous
5. Perambulation
6. Contrary
7. Invocation
8. Narration
9. Nautical
10. Patriotic

Exercise 3. 12
Revision. Translate the following:
1. sub aquā
2. post fābulam
3. ante pugnam
4. in īnsulīs
5. cum incolīs
6. inter agricolās
7. sine sagittīs
8. per viam
9. dē Troiā
10. prope Rōmam

Using Latin

inter
An inter-city train is one which travels between cities.
In Latin, inter = between.

The Foundation of Rome

You will remember that Romulus and Remus drove the wicked king Amulius from the throne and put their old grandfather, Numitor, in his place. After this little excitement they felt they needed a kingdom of their own. They set off to the place where Faustulus had first found them in the she-wolf's cave. This would make a good place for a new city, they thought, but who should be king? The two twins looked around at the seven hills, rising above them. Then, deciding to rely on augury (a form of fortune-telling, using signs or omens from the natural world) for the answer to their problem, Romulus climbed the Palatine Hill and Remus climbed the Aventine. There they waited to see what the birds would tell them.

After a while Remus got all excited when he saw six vultures, flying across the sky above him. Taking this to be a good omen, he ran down the hill and up the Palatine to tell his brother. However, when he got there Romulus said that he had seen twelve vultures and so it was decided that the city should be called Rome after its first king, Romulus.

A few days later, Remus, who was quite sulky about the outcome of the bird-watching spree, jumped over a wall which was in the process of being built around the city. His brother was not impressed and killed Remus with the words 'thus perish anyone who jumps over my walls!'

So you really want to learn Latin...

Exercise 3. 13

Read the information on the left-hand page about the foundation of Rome and then answer the following questions in complete sentences:

1. When did Romulus and Remus decide to build a new city?
2. Where did they think would make a suitable place for the new city?
3. How did they plan to resolve the question of who should be king?
4. Which hill did Romulus climb?
5. Which hill did Remus climb?
6. Why did Remus think that the omens had proved favourable to him?
7. Why did this prove not to be the case?
8. Why was the city of Rome called Rome?
9. What do you think it might have been called had Remus been its first king?
10. What happened to Remus in the end?

Using Latin

per cent
Per cent (or percent) is short for per centum = through a hundred.

CHAPTER 4
The 2nd conjugation; the 2nd declension

Verbs of the 2nd conjugation: moneō

All the verbs you have met so far have been 1st conjugation, going like amō. The next type of verb to cope with belongs to the 2nd conjugation and goes like moneō = *I warn* or *advise*.

Moneō uses exactly the same endings as amō, but instead of having a present stem ending in -ā it has one ending in -ē.

moneō, monēre, monuī, monitum = I warn / advise

Present Tense

mone-ō	I warn
monē-s	You warn
mone-t	He, she, it warns
monē-mus	We warn
monē-tis	You warn
mone-nt	They warn

Imperfect Tense

monē-bam	I was warning
monē-bās	etc.
monē-bat	
monē-bāmus	
monē-bātis	
monē-bant	

Future Tense

monē-bō	I shall / will warn
monē-bis	etc.
monē-bit	
monē-bimus	
monē-bitis	
monē-bunt	

Perfect Tense

monu-ī	I have warned
monu-istī	etc.
monu-it	
monu-imus	
monu-istis	
monu-ērunt	

Principal parts: 2nd conjugation

Verbs like moneō have principal parts which tend to go -eō, -ēre, -uī, -itum. It is the fact that the 2nd principal parts goes -ēre (to rhyme, roughly, with hairy) that tells us the verb is 2nd conjugation. The present stem is found, as usual, by going to the second principal part and chopping off the -re. The perfect tense is formed by adding the normal perfect tense endings to the perfect stem (found, as normal, in the 3rd principal part).

Regular 2nd conjugation verbs go -uī, -itum in the 3rd and 4th principal parts but many do not. For example videō, vidēre, vīdī, vīsum = *I see* is 2nd conjugation (because it goes -eō, -ēre) but its 3rd and 4th principal parts are irregular. Clearly with verbs such as this you have to learn the principal parts very carefully.

So you really want to learn Latin...

Exercise 4. 1
Study the information on the left-hand page about the 2nd conjugation. Then, using the verbs given below, write out the following tenses:
1. Present tense of moneō, monēre, monuī, monitum = I warn
2. Future tense of terreō, terrēre, terruī, territum = I terrify
3. Imperfect tense of habeō, habēre, habuī, habitum = I have
4. Perfect tense of dēbeō, dēbēre, dēbuī, dēbitum = I owe

Exercise 4. 2
Using the vocabulary at the back of the book, translate into Latin:
1. He was teaching
2. They see
3. We shall fear
4. She will hold
5. You (pl.) do not fear
6. To teach
7. They have warned
8. He has terrified
9. You (sing.) have held
10. We do not fear

Exercise 4. 3
Translate into English:
1. timēbat
2. docēbunt
3. nōn docuistis
4. monēbit
5. habēre et tenēre
6. tenet
7. monuērunt
8. timēre
9. tenēbātis
10. habēbimus

Exercise 4. 4
Study the information on the left-hand page about principal parts. 1st conjugation verbs can be recognised by their first two principal parts, which always go -ō, -āre. 2nd conjugation verbs always go -eō, -ēre.
To which conjugation do the following verbs belong? Write them out in the present tense.
1. maneō, manēre, mānsī, mānsum = I remain
2. cēlō, cēlāre, cēlāvī, cēlātum = I hide
3. dēleō, dēlēre, dēlēvī, dēlētum = I destroy
4. vītō, vītāre, vītāvī, vītātum = I avoid
5. sedeō, sedēre, sēdī, sessum = I sit

Using Latin

etc.
etc. stands for et cētera = and the rest.

Nouns of the 2nd declension: annus

All the nouns you have met so far have been 1st declension nouns like mēnsa. It is now time to bring on the 2nd declension. There are a number of types to learn, but the most important is shown below.

2nd declension nouns in -us go like annus = a year. They are almost always masculine.

annus, annī, m. = year		
Nom.	ann-us	Year (subject)
Voc.	ann-e	O year (addressing)
Acc.	ann-um	Year (object)
Gen.	ann-ī	Of a year
Dat.	ann-ō	To, for a year
Abl.	ann-ō	By, with or from a year
Nom.	ann-ī	Years (subject)
Voc.	ann-ī	O years (addressing)
Acc.	ann-ōs	Years (object)
Gen.	ann-ōrum	Of the years
Dat.	ann-īs	To, for the years
Abl.	ann-īs	By, with or from the years

Stems and endings

2nd declension nouns always have a genitive singular ending in -ī. The stem of a noun can be found by looking at the genitive singular and chopping off the ending. Thus the genitive singular of annus is annī. If we take off the -ī ending we are left with the stem ann-.

Sometimes care needs to be taken to get the correct stem. For example the Latin for a sword is gladius, which has the genitive singular gladiī (with two 'i's). If we take off the -ī ending from this, we are left with gladi-. Where a noun has a stem ending in -i, you just have to put up with the fact that this will sometimes lead to your getting two 'i's together (e.g. gladiī and gladiīs).

A word of caution

In this chapter you have been dealt the double blow of being told that not all verbs go like amō and not all nouns go like mēnsa. The 2nd conjugation (moneō) and the 2nd declension (annus) have crept up to make your life tricky.

From now on, then, when working with nouns and verbs, make sure you know which sort they are before trying to add endings to them. Until further notice, nouns ending in -a must go like mēnsa; nouns in -us go like annus. Don't try to put mēnsa endings on annus nouns or annus endings on mēnsa nouns. They don't like it!

So you really want to learn Latin...

Exercise 4. 5
Study the information on the left-hand page about 2nd declension nouns like annus and stems and endings. Notice how, just as with mēnsa, the endings are added to the noun stem. Write out in full the following nouns. Be careful with the double 'i's in nūntius. And beware, not all of these go like annus.
1. annus, annī, m. = year
2. dominus, dominī, m. = lord, master
3. locus, locī, m. = place
4. victōria, victōriae, f. = victory
5. servus, servī, m. = slave

Exercise 4. 6
Give the Latin for, using prepositions where necessary:
1. Of the lord
2. Near the place
3. For the messenger
4. Without a lord
5. Towards the place
6. Of the years
7. With the master
8. Around the place
9. O messengers
10. Towards the messenger

Exercise 4. 7
Translate into English:
1. ad locum
2. ante victōriam
3. in locō
4. inter incolās
5. sine aquā
6. nūntiōrum
7. cum nūntiīs
8. domine
9. circum mēnsam
10. prope locum

Exercise 4. 8
Read the word of caution on the left-hand page. Then translate into Latin. Some of the nouns are 1st declension, some are 2nd declension. Remember to use the correct endings with the different declensions.
1. The slaves fear the master.
2. The women were teaching the slaves.
3. The master will prepare the place for the inhabitants.
4. The slaves have prepared the ground for the master.
5. The messengers tell a story to the slave.

Using Latin

AD
AD stands for annō Dominī = in the year of our Lord.

Nouns like bellum

The other main type of 2nd declension noun goes like bellum = war. Nouns that end in -um go like bellum and are neuter, i.e. neither masculine nor feminine. The main difficulty with neuter nouns is that there is no difference between their nominative, vocative and accusative cases, so working out whether a noun is the subject or the object is that much more difficult. (It is also possible to muddle the -a ending of a neuter noun with the -a ending of a 1st declension noun like mēnsa, but only if you haven't learnt your vocabulary properly.)

bellum, bellī, n. = war

Nom.	bell-um	War (subject)
Voc.	bell-um	O war (addressing)
Acc.	bell-um	War (object)
Gen.	bell-ī	Of a war
Dat.	bell-ō	To, for a war
Abl.	bell-ō	By, with or from a war
Nom.	bell-a	Wars (subject)
Voc.	bell-a	O wars (addressing)
Acc.	bell-a	Wars (object)
Gen.	bell-ōrum	Of the wars
Dat.	bell-īs	To, for the wars
Abl.	bell-īs	By, with or from the wars

Working with neuters

So how do we cope then? We see the ending -um but can no longer be sure that this is an accusative singular ending (as it would be for annus type nouns). Again, we fall back on common sense and, of course, obeying the rules of translation carefully.

```
        ?         V
e.g. bellum  nōn  amat.   = He does not love the war.
```

(**Common sense**: bellum could have been nominative, but *the war does not love* makes no sense!)

```
        ?         O         V
e.g. tēlum  servum  vulnerat.   = The spear wounds the slave.
```

(**N.B.** tēlum could be nominative or accusative. But servum could only be accusative, because it goes like annus. So if servum is the object, tēlum must be the subject.)

So you really want to learn Latin…

Exercise 4. 9

Study the information on the left-hand page about nouns like bellum. Then write out the following nouns in full. (Take care with the stem of auxilium.)

1. tēlum, tēlī, n. = spear
2. dōnum, dōnī, n. = gift
3. auxilium, auxiliī, n. = help
4. perīculum, perīculī, n. = danger

Exercise 4. 10

Study the information on the left-hand page about working with neuters. Then translate the following into English:

1. agricola tēlum portābat.
2. dōnum servus amābit.
3. nūntium dominī vocābās.
4. tēlum dominī servum vulnerābat.
5. tēla dominī incolās vulnerābunt.
6. incola tēla ad dominum portāvit.
7. nautae tēla prope aquam tenēbant.
8. tēla et dōna ad incolās īnsulae portābimus.
9. incolās auxiliō agricolārum superābant.
10. dominus servōs dē tēlīs monuit.

Exercise 4. 11

Translate into Latin:

1. The master of the country has warned the slaves.
2. Master, we do not fear the dangers of war.
3. The woman will overcome the slaves with a spear.
4. O master, we do not fear the spears of the slaves!
5. The woman was hurrying towards the farmers.
6. The farmers were holding the gifts of the woman.
7. O woman, we have carried the gifts from the land of Troy.
8. Farmers, I do not like gifts!
9. The sailors have attacked the town with spears.
10. With the help of the slaves, the farmers have overcome the inhabitants.

Using Latin

P.S.
The letters P.S. stand for post scrīptum = written after.

Dealing with the simple past

We have seen that the imperfect tense (e.g. amābat) can mean *he was loving* or *he used to love*, and that the perfect tense (e.g. amāvit) means *he has loved*. But what if we wish to use the simple past, e.g. *he loved*, or *he warned*, or *he walked*? Or *he did not love, did not warn* or *did not walk*. Which tense do we use for this?

1. If we wish to refer to an action, completed at some definite point of time in the past, we are using a tense sometimes called the *aorist*. This tense (very common in Greek) did not have its own set of endings in Latin and was forced to borrow the perfect tense endings.
   E.g. The girl *gave* a gift to the farmer. = puella dōnum agricolae dedit.
   E.g. She *did not give* a gift to the farmer. = dōnum agricolae nōn dedit.

2. However, if we are referring to a continuous or incomplete action in the past, we use the imperfect tense.
   E.g. The girl *remained* on the island. = puella in īnsulā manēbat.

Vocabulary 4

Nouns in -us		Verbs	
annus, annī, m.	year	cēlō, -āre, -āvī, -ātum	I hide
dominus, dominī, m.	lord, master	dō[2], dăre, dedī, dătum	I give
locus[1], locī, m.	place	dēleō, -ēre, dēlēvī, dēlētum	I destroy
nūntius, nūntiī, m.	messenger, message	doceō, -ēre, docuī, doctum	I teach
		habeō, -ēre, -uī, -itum	I have
servus, servī, m.	slave	maneō, -ēre, mānsī, mānsum	I remain
Nouns in -um			
auxilium, auxiliī, n.	help	moneō, -ēre, -uī, -itum	I warn, advise
bellum, bellī, n.	war	sedeō, -ēre, sēdī, sessum	I sit
dōnum, dōnī, n.	gift	teneō, -ēre, tenuī, tentum	I hold
perīculum, perīculī, n.	danger	timeō, -ēre, -uī [3]	I fear
tēlum, telī, n.	spear		

1. locus is a 2nd declension noun like annus, but it has an alternative neuter plural form (loca) which goes like the plural of bellum.
2. dō is a very strange verb going, for the sake of argument, like amō (dō, dās, dat, dămus, dătis, dant; dăbō, dăbis, etc.). Note its strange 3rd principal part and the fact that, apart from in the 2nd person singular of the present tense (and in something called the singular imperative), it is pronounced with a short a.
3. timeō has no supine. Some verbs don't. Don't worry about it. *You* don't have a supine and you cope!

So you really want to learn Latin...

Exercise 4. 12

So you are now more than ready to face your first passage for translation. A passage is simply a collection of sentences joined up into a continuous story. There is nothing difficult about it, whether you are translating into Latin or out of Latin. All the same rules apply. So, read the note about dealing with the simple past on the left-hand page and then translate the following passage into English, writing your translation on alternate lines.

agricola fābulam nārrābat: 'incolae Graeciae cum incolīs Troiae pugnābant. Troiam nōn dēlēvērunt. incolae Troiae incolās Graeciae timēbant sed incolās Graeciae multīs sagittīs et tēlīs vulnerābant.

  'prope Troiam habitābam et in bellō pugnābam. multa tēla habēbam et in pugnīs pugnābam. sed sagittās sub mēnsā cēlāvī. incolae Graeciae sagittās timēbant. incolae Graeciae agricolās Troiae superāvērunt et terram dēlēvērunt. post victōriam, incolae Graeciae prope mēnsam sedēbant. sub mensā cum sagittīs sedēbam. incolās vulnerāvī et auxiliō sagittārum incolās superāvī.'

  agricola fābulam multīs incolīs Rōmae nārrāvit. incolae fābulam nōn amāvērunt!

Exercise 4. 13

Translate the following passage into Latin. Take care over which Latin tense to use to translate the English simple past.

A woman was giving gifts to a girl. The girl did not like the woman but she liked the gifts. She sat near the woman and told a story to the woman.

  'A slave was living on an island. He did not have water. He called the inhabitants of the island but they were working. He hurried along the streets and called a sailor. The sailor looked at the slave. The slave looked at the sailor. The sailor had water. He was not giving the water to the slave. The slave overcame the sailor with a spear and carried the water along the streets.'

  The woman did not like the story; but the girl liked the gifts!

Exercise 4. 14

From which Latin words do the following derive? Explain the meaning of the English words and translate the Latin ones.

1. Monitor
2. Delete
3. Session
4. Annual
5. Auxiliary
6. Dominate
7. Donation
8. Location
9. Servile
10. Bellicose

Using Latin

interim
interim = meanwhile. E.g. the train was late so, in the interim, he read his book.

The Sabine women

Rome quickly filled up with all Romulus's shepherd friends and a group of criminals, who came seeking sanctuary from the law in their own cities. But there weren't many women. In fact there weren't any.

Romulus invited girls from the neighbouring tribes to come to Rome but, as you might imagine, their parents weren't too keen. So he devised a cunning plan. He organised a festival in the city at which there was to be feasting and games and invited all the neighbouring people to come and watch. Eager to see the new city and to partake in the festivities, hundreds of men, particularly from the nearby Sabine tribe, came to Rome, bringing with them their wives and daughters. At a given signal, Romulus's men seized the women and carried them off to make them their wives. The men, who had come unarmed, were forced to flee.

Festivals

Festivals were held in the ancient world at regular intervals, often to coincide with the full moon. The earliest festivals were probably associated with the celebration of the harvest and, although the main purpose was to perform worship to the gods, games, feasting and markets were soon added. It is easy to imagine how the Sabine people would have been attracted to the festival in the new city of Rome by the prospect of a day or two of high-class entertainment.

The most famous festivals started in Greece, including the festival of Olympia at which the Olympic games began. An important part of such festivals would have been the animal sacrifices, made as an offering to the gods and giving the people an opportunity to feast on the meat. Processions, too, would have enabled the people to parade through their town in all their finery, rather like a modern-day carnival.

So you really want to learn Latin...

Exercise 4. 15

Read the information about the Sabine women and festivals and then answer the following questions in complete sentences:
1. Describe the population of Rome before the arrival of the women.
2. What did Romulus do to try to increase the female population in the city?
3. Why do you think this was unsuccessful?
4. Why did Romulus think that organising a festival might prove more successful?
5. What forms of entertainment might have been organised at this festival?
6. From which nearby tribe did most of the visitors come to see the games?
7. What did Romulus's men do at the given signal?
8. How do you think the Sabine women felt at being carried off in this way?

Revision

At this stage you might like to check what you have and what you have not mastered. You should know *by heart* the following:
- amō and moneō: principal parts and 4 tenses
- mēnsa, annus and bellum: singular and plural
- names and meanings of the 6 cases

You should also have learnt all the words in Vocabularies 1-4, and should be able to recognise them *both ways*, i.e. know what teneō means **and** know the Latin for *I hold*.

prō fōrmā
prō fōrmā = for form. For example a prō fōrmā application is one that follows a particular form.

CHAPTER 5
Adjectives; more on the 2nd declension

Adjectives like bonus

An adjective is used to describe a noun and must 'agree' with the noun it describes in gender, case and number. For example, if the *noun* is feminine, genitive singular, the *adjective* must be feminine, genitive singular.

Adjectives, therefore, like nouns, need to have cases. But the good news is that you already know all the endings you need. Bonus is a 1st/2nd declension adjective and as you can see, it takes its endings from the nouns of the 1st and 2nd declensions which you have already learnt:

bonus, bona, bonum = good

	Masculine	Feminine	Neuter
Nom.	bon-us	bon-a	bon-um
Voc.	bon-e	bon-a	bon-um
Acc.	bon-um	bon-am	bon-um
Gen.	bon-ī	bon-ae	bon-ī
Dat.	bon-ō	bon-ae	bon-ō
Abl.	bon-ō	bon-ā	bon-ō
Nom.	bon-ī	bon-ae	bon-a
Voc.	bon-ī	bon-ae	bon-a
Acc.	bon-ōs	bon-ās	bon-a
Gen.	bon-ōrum	bon-ārum	bon-ōrum
Dat.	bon-īs	bon-īs	bon-īs
Abl.	bon-īs	bon-īs	bon-īs

Agreement of adjectives

An adjective must 'agree' with the noun it describes. Adjectives in Latin often come after their nouns, so when translating into Latin, do the noun first; then work out which gender, case and number the noun is; then select that form of the adjective.

- e.g. Of the master = dominī
  Masculine, genitive singular
  Of the **good** master = dominī **bonī**

- e.g. For the sailor = nautae
  Masculine, dative singular
  For the **good** sailor = nautae **bonō**

So you really want to learn Latin...

Exercise 5. 1
Study the information on the left-hand page about adjectives. Adjectives ending in -us go like bonus and are always listed with their masculine, feminine and neuter endings. E.g. multus, multa, multum (or multus, -a, -um) = much, many. Give the following:
1. Masc. acc. pl. of malus, -a, -um = bad
2. Fem. dat. sing. of fessus, -a, -um = tired
3. Neut. abl. pl. of īrātus, -a, -um = angry
4. Masc. nom. pl. of longus, -a, -um = long
5. Fem. gen. sing. of magnus, -a, -um = big, great

Exercise 5. 2
Study the information on the left-hand page about the agreement of adjectives. Work out which gender, case and number the following nouns are. Then make bonus agree with them.
1. mēnsās
2. nautam
3. agricolam
4. perīculum
5. puellārum
6. servōrum
7. bellī
8. domine
9. dominōs
10. tēlī

Exercise 5. 3
Give the Latin for, using prepositions where necessary:
1. In great danger
2. Of the bad slave
3. O good sailors!
4. Out of the big island
5. For the tired farmer
6. In the great battle
7. With the good inhabitants
8. Under the long tables
9. Along the long road
10. Of the angry girls

Exercise 5. 4
Study the following sentences. To ensure correct translation, brackets may be placed around the nouns and adjectives that go together (as in the first three sentences). Then translate into English.
1. [dominus īrātus] [servum malum] vocāvit.
2. [agricolae fessī] terram parābant.
3. [multī agricolae] incolam [tēlīs longīs] superābant.
4. dominī malī servōs fessōs nōn amant.
5. incolās tēlīs magnīs et multīs sagittīs superābant.

Using Latin

bonus
A bonus is a benefit or good thing. The word bonus is simply the Latin for good.

Puer and magister

You have met the two main types of 2nd declension noun: annus and bellum. Now there are two more types to learn, both very similar.

	puer, puerī, m. = boy	**magister, magistrī, m. = master**
Nom.	puer	magister
Voc.	puer	magister
Acc.	puer-um	magistr-um
Gen.	puer-ī	magistr-ī
Dat.	puer-ō	magistr-ō
Abl.	puer-ō	magistr-ō
Nom.	puer-ī	magistr-ī
Voc.	puer-ī	magistr-ī
Acc.	puer-ōs	magistr-ōs
Gen.	puer-ōrum	magistr-ōrum
Dat.	puer-īs	magistr-īs
Abl.	puer-īs	magistr-īs

These nouns use identical endings to annus except in the nominative and vocative singular. The difference between the two is that nouns like puer keep their e whereas nouns like magister drop their e.

You have already learnt how to find a noun's stem by looking at its genitive singular. If the -er of the nominative has changed to -erī, then the noun goes like puer. But if the -er has changed to -rī (in other words if the e has dropped out), it goes like magister.

E.g. ager, agrī, m. = field goes like magister, because it has dropped its e.

So you really want to learn Latin...

Exercise 5. 5

Study the information on the left-hand page about nouns like puer and magister. Nouns like puer are quite rare (apart from puer itself), so if in doubt, drop the e!
Write out in full:

1. liber, librī, m. = book
2. ager, agrī, m. = field

Exercise 5. 6

Translate into English. As before, put brackets around the nouns and adjectives that go together before starting. Where there are prepositions, you may find you have to put a bracket around *three* words: the preposition, its noun and an adjective agreeing with the noun.

e.g. puella [ad agricolam bonum] ambulat. = the girl walks towards the good farmer.

1. [magister bonus] [puerum fessum] vocāvit.
2. puerōs [dē bellō magnō] docēbō.
3. bella magna puer bonus nōn amat.
4. in agrōs magnōs cum servīs festīnāvit.
5. magister īrātus puerum et servōs spectāvit.
6. puerōs malōs nōn docēbō.
7. agricola magnus in agrō labōrābat.
8. puerum et servōs tēlō longō superāvit.
9. puer et servī cum agricolā malō pugnābant.
10. magister puerō auxilium nōn dedit.

Exercise 5. 7

Translate the following into Latin:

An angry farmer was walking along the road. He was watching a boy. The boy was telling a story to a woman. The farmer hurried towards the boy and shouted. 'Boy, you are sitting in my field.' The boy was sitting on the ground. He remained in the place but he was hiding a spear. 'Farmer, I will sit in the field.' The woman was afraid but the boy remained in the place. The angry farmer walked along the long road towards the boy, but the boy overcame the farmer.

Using Latin

media
media = things in the middle. Newspapers, T.V., etc. are in the middle between us and the events being reported.

Adjectives in -er

Just as some 2nd declension nouns end in -er rather than -us, so do some adjectives. And just as some nouns drop the e and some don't, so it is with adjectives.

tener, tenera, tenerum = tender

	M.	F.	N.
Nom.	tener	tener-a	tener-um
Voc.	tener	tener-a	tener-um
Acc.	tener-um	tener-am	tener-um
Gen.	tener-ī	tener-ae	tener-ī
Dat.	tener-ō	tener-ae	tener-ō
Abl.	tener-ō	tener-ā	tener-ō
Nom.	tener-ī	tener-ae	tener-a
Voc.	tener-ī	tener-ae	tener-a
Acc.	tener-ōs	tener-ās	tener-a
Gen.	tener-ōrum	tener-ārum	tener-ōrum
Dat.	tener-īs	tener-īs	tener-īs
Abl.	tener-īs	tener-īs	tener-īs

pulcher, pulchra, pulchrum = beautiful

	M.	F.	N.
Nom.	pulcher	pulchr-a	pulchr-um
Voc.	pulcher	pulchr-a	pulchr-um
Acc.	pulchr-um	pulchr-am	pulchr-um
Gen.	pulchr-ī	pulchr-ae	pulchr-ī
Dat.	pulchr-ō	pulchr-ae	pulchr-ō
Abl.	pulchr-ō	pulchr-ā	pulchr-ō
Nom.	pulchr-ī	pulchr-ae	pulchr-a
Voc.	pulchr-ī	pulchr-ae	pulchr-a
Acc.	pulchr-ōs	pulchr-ās	pulchr-a
Gen.	pulchr-ōrum	pulchr-ārum	pulchr-ōrum
Dat.	pulchr-īs	pulchr-īs	pulchr-īs
Abl.	pulchr-īs	pulchr-īs	pulchr-īs

You can tell whether an adjective in -er goes like tener or pulcher by studying its feminine and neuter forms, to see whether the e has dropped or not.

E.g. miser, misera, miserum = wretched: goes like tener;
    noster, nostra, nostrum = our: goes like pulcher.

So you really want to learn Latin...

Exercise 5. 8
Study the information on the left-hand page about adjectives in -er. Note how you can tell whether the adjective in -er goes like tener or pulcher by studying its feminine and neuter forms to see whether the e has dropped out or not. Remember also that adjectives in -us go like bonus. Give the following forms:

1. Masc. gen. sing. of vester, vestra, vestrum = your (of you (plural))
2. Fem. dat. pl. of noster, nostra, nostrum = our
3. Neut. gen. pl. of miser, misera, miserum = wretched, miserable
4. Fem. abl. sing. of meus, mea, meum = my

Exercise 5. 9
Translate into Latin:

1. The wretched farmer
2. My daughter
3. The beautiful gifts
4. Of the tender girls
5. With our arrows
6. O inhabitants of Troy, we looked at the beautiful land.
7. By our wisdom we have overcome the inhabitants of Greece.
8. We will call the tired messengers.
9. The tired sailors sail around the beautiful island.
10. You will not overcome our country with arrows and spears.

Exercise 5. 10
Translate into English:

1. magistrī nostrī puellās fessās monuērunt.
2. puerī librōs longōs nōn tenēbant.
3. puerī, librōs ad mēnsam magistrī portābitis.
4. librōs ad mēnsam magnam nōn portābimus.
5. magistrī fābulās puellīs nārrābant.
6. puellae fābulās amābant sed magistrōs timēbant.
7. puella mala librum sub mēnsā cēlāvit.
8. magister puellam pulchram exspectāvit.
9. puellās malās nōn amō.
10. puellae et puerī ē locō ambulāvērunt et in agrōs festīnāvērunt.

festīnā lentē
festīnā lentē = hurry slowly! It is the Latin equivalent for 'less haste, more speed!'

Vocabulary 5

Adjectives in -us		Adjectives in -er	
bonus, -a, -um	good	miser, misera, miserum	miserable
fessus, -a, -um	tired	noster, nostra, nostrum	our
īrātus -a, -um	angry	pulcher, pulchra, pulchrum	beautiful
longus, -a, -um	long	tener, tenera, tenerum	tender
magnus, -a, -um	big, great	vester, vestra, vestrum	your [2]
malus, -a, -um	bad	**Nouns**	
meus, -a, -um	my [1]	ager, agrī, m.	field
multus, -a, -um	much, many	castra, castrōrum, n. pl.	camp
tuus, -a, -um	your [2]	cōpiae, cōpiārum, f. pl.	forces
		liber, librī, m.	book
		magister, magistrī, m.	master
		puer, puerī, m.	boy

1. meus has vocative masculine singular mī.
   E.g. ō mī amīce.
2. tuus = belonging to you (sing.); vester = belonging to you (pl.).
   E.g. O farmer, you love your country. = agricola, patriam tuam amās.
   E.g. O girls, you love your country. = puellae, patriam vestram amātis.

Plural nouns

Some nouns in Latin are only found in the plural.

1. castra, castrōrum, n. pl. = a camp, is really the plural of the neuter noun castrum = a fort. But it is always used in the plural to mean a camp.
   E.g. He looked at the camp. = castra spectāvit.
   Do not try to make castra decline like mēnsa (just because it ends in -a). It goes like bellum in the plural.
2. cōpiae, cōpiārum, f. pl. = forces, is really the plural of the feminine noun cōpia = a supply. But it is used in the plural to mean forces (i.e. military forces, troops).
   E.g. He overcame the forces. = cōpiās superāvit.

Other modern languages

Once you have got the hang of spotting English derivations, you can while away the hours spotting French, Spanish, and Italian ones. Notice how the spelling changes from language to language, but the Latin root is always clear. Notice, also, how English very often has a word which is clearly not derived from Latin (*carry* does not come from portō) and yet has associated words (*portable*) which clearly are:

Latin	English	French	Spanish	Italian
portāre	portable	porter	(trans)portar	portare

So you really want to learn Latin...

Exercise 5. 11

Study Vocabulary 5 and the information given underneath about tuus, vester and plural nouns. Then translate the following into Latin. You will have to concentrate on the *yours* to get them right. (N.B. names such as Romulus are not given in the vocabulary. For the time being, names in -a go like mēnsa, names in -us go like annus.)

1. We love our country.
2. They love my stories.
3. O master, we do not like your books.
4. O masters, we do not like your books.
5. Our forces built a big camp near the water.
6. O Romulus, your forces have overcome the inhabitants of the country.
7. O girls, you have hidden your books under your table.
8. O Romulus, the inhabitants of my country have overcome your forces.
9. We will prepare a camp in the big field of the angry farmer.
10. You (sing.) have warned your masters.

Exercise 5. 12

Read the information on the left-hand page about other modern languages. Copy and complete the table of derivations below, using as many modern languages as you can.

LATIN	ENGLISH	FRENCH	SPANISH	ITALIAN
portāre				
amāre				
dōnum				
amīcus				
annus				

Exercise 5. 13

Revision. *Without looking up*, translate:

1. He destroys
2. We fear
3. You (sing.) hide
4. We remain
5. They give
6. War
7. A year
8. The spears
9. With help
10. Of the gift
11. The slaves
12. In danger
13. After the stories
14. With the woman
15. Through the street
16. Concerning Rome
17. Out of the country
18. Into the street
19. In the water
20. Against the inhabitants

Using Latin

exit
An exit is a way out.
In Latin exit = he/she/it goes out.

The first Roman traitress

Titus Tatius, the king of the Sabines, was not a happy cookie when he saw how the Romans had tricked his people into losing their women-folk. So he got an army together and attacked. The Romans defended their city from a citadel on the Capitoline hill. One evening Tarpeia, the daughter of one of the Roman commanders, went outside the city walls to fetch water. On the way she met a group of Sabine soldiers wearing gold bracelets and rings on their left hands. Tarpeia badly wanted the bracelets and rings and offered to escort the Sabines into the city in return for 'what the soldiers were wearing on their left hands'.

That night Tarpeia let the soldiers into the city. As they passed the greedy traitress they kept their promise by throwing their shields, which they had in their left hands, on top of the poor girl. And that was the end of her.

So you really want to learn Latin...

Exercise 5. 14

Read the story about the first Roman traitress on the left-hand page. Then answer the following questions in complete sentences:

1. Who was Titus Tatius?
2. Why was Titus not a happy cookie?
3. What did he do to put things right?
4. Who was Tarpeia?
5. How did she come to be outside the city walls?
6. Whom did she meet?
7. What did Tarpeia like about the way the soldiers were dressed?
8. What was her offer to the soldiers and why was this treacherous?
9. How did the enemy soldiers keep their promise to Tarpeia?
10. What do you think the moral of this story is?

Using Latin

ex librīs
This is often used on book plates.
ex librīs = out of the books.

CHAPTER 6

The 3rd and 4th conjugations; questions

So now to finish off the verbs. We have met amō and moneō, and learnt to tell them apart by studying their principal parts. Verbs in -ō, -āre go like amō; verbs in -eō, -ēre go like moneō.

Verbs like regō

Verbs of the 3rd conjugation go like regō. The endings for regō are similar to those which you have met before, but there are significant differences which should be noted carefully. You will soon learn that regō is a pig and will try to be awkward whenever possible.

rego, regere, rēxī, rēctum = I rule

Present Tense		Imperfect Tense	
reg-ō	I rule	reg-ēbam	I was ruling
reg-is	You rule	reg-ēbās	etc.
reg-it	He, she, it rules	reg-ēbat	
reg-imus	We rule	reg-ēbāmus	
reg-itis	You rule	reg-ēbātis	
reg-unt	They rule	reg-ēbant	
Future Tense		**Perfect Tense**	
reg-am	I shall / will rule	rēx-ī	I have ruled
reg-ēs	etc.	rēx-istī	etc.
reg-et		rēx-it	
reg-ēmus		rēx-imus	
reg-ētis		rēx-istis	
reg-ent		rēx-ērunt	

Problems with regō

1. The present stem of regō is found in the 2nd principal part by chopping off -ere (rather than just -re as is normal).
2. The future tense of regō goes -am, -ēs, -et, rather than -bō, -bis, -bit.
3. The 2nd principal part of regō ends in -ere, just like the 2nd principal part of moneō. The difference is that verbs like regō go -ō, -ere, whereas verbs like moneo go -eō, -ēre. The ē of monēre is pronounced long (to rhyme – almost – with hairy), whereas in regere it is short.
4. The last two principal parts of verbs like regō follow no particular pattern and just have to be learnt.

Apart from that, regō is fine...!

So you really want to learn Latin...

Exercise 6. 1
Study the information on the left-hand page about verbs like regō, especially the problems with regō. Notice how the principal parts of these verbs go -ō, -ere (not to be confused with -eō, -ēre). Write out the present tense of the following. They do not all go like regō!
1. cadō, cadere, cecidī, cāsum = I fall
2. surgō, surgere, surrēxī, surrēctum = I rise, get up
3. clāmō, clāmāre, clāmāvī, clāmātum = I shout
4. terreō, terrēre, terruī, territum = I terrify, frighten

Exercise 6. 2
Write out in the future tense:
1. cadō
2. surgō
3. clāmō
4. terreō

Exercise 6. 3
Write out in the imperfect tense:
1. currō, currere, cucurrī, cursum = I run
2. gerō, gerere, gessī, gestum = I conduct, I wear
3. scrībō, scrībere, scrīpsī, scrīptum = I write
4. dūcō, dūcere, dūxī, ductum = I lead

Exercise 6. 4
Write out in the perfect tense. Be sure to use the 3rd principal part of the verbs. Notice how verbs like regō have no particular pattern for the perfect stem (one of the reasons why regō is a pig!).
1. currō
2. gerō
3. clāmō
4. cadō
5. dūcō

alibī
If someone uses an alibi, it shows they were somewhere else. In Latin, alibī = elsewhere.

Questions in Latin

There are three ways of asking a question in Latin:

1. Using a questioning word, such as quis = who? quid = what? cūr = why? or ubĭ = where?
   E.g. Why are you running? = cūr curris?
   E.g. Who is running? = quis currit?

2. Putting -ne on the end of the first word in the sentence.
   E.g. Are you running? = currisne?

3. Using nōnne or num. Nōnne is used to ask a question expecting the answer 'yes'; num is used to ask a question expecting the answer 'no'.
   E.g. You are running, aren't you? = nōnne curris?
   E.g. You are not running, are you? = num curris?

-ne, nōnne, num: points to note

-ne, nōnne and num can be used at your discretion, depending on whether you feel the expected answer is 'yes' (nōnne), 'no' (num) or whether it could be either of these (-ne).
E.g. Are you afraid? =

(a) timēsne? (if you simply want to know whether the person is afraid or not);

(b) nōnne timēs? (if you think it is likely that the person is afraid);

(c) num timēs? (if you think it unlikely that the person is afraid).

As in English, this sort of variation could have been achieved with the tone of voice, as Julius Caesar demonstrated in 44 B.C.!

'Et tū, Brūte?'

So you really want to learn Latin...

Exercise 6. 5
Study the information on the left-hand page about questions in Latin. Then translate into English:
1. cūr in agrīs ambulābās?
2. ambulāsne in agrīs?
3. nōnne in agrīs ambulābis?
4. num in agrīs ambulāvistī?
5. quis puerōs docēbit?
6. ubi labōrābātis, agricolae?
7. quis incolās patriae regit?
8. nōnne magister puerōs et puellās docēbit?
9. num puerī et puellae magistrum amant?
10. cōpiāsne sagittīs et tēlīs superābimus?

Exercise 6. 6
Translate into Latin:
1. Does the farmer love the girl?
2. Will the sailor sail to the island?
3. Will the master teach the boys?
4. The master has not hidden the book, has he?
5. We will overcome the inhabitants of Italy, won't we?
6. Why is the tired farmer remaining in the field?
7. Where will you hide the girl's book?
8. Are the slaves preparing the master's table?
9. Have the slaves prepared the water for the woman?
10. The forces of Troy will not overcome the inhabitants, will they?

Exercise 6. 7
From which Latin words do the following English words derive? Explain the meaning of the English words and translate the Latin ones.
1. Miserable
2. Agriculture
3. Multiply
4. Copious
5. Irate
6. Annual
7. Delete
8. Dominate
9. Sedentary
10. Portable

rota
'They have arranged to do the washing-up on a rota.'
The word rota is the Latin for a wheel.

Verbs like audiō

Verbs of the 4th conjugation go like audiō. Audiō is very similar to regō, copying the spelling (although not the pronunciation) of its endings almost exactly. Verbs like audiō have principal parts which go -iō, -īre. The present stem is found in the second principal part by chopping off -re (audī-).

audiō, audīre, audīvī, audītum = I hear

Present Tense		Imperfect Tense	
audi-ō	I hear	audi-ēbam	I was hearing
audī-s	You hear	audi-ēbās	etc.
audi-t	He, she, it hears	audi-ēbat	
audī-mus	We hear	audi-ēbāmus	
audī-tis	You hear	audi-ēbātis	
audi-unt	They hear	audi-ēbant	
Future Tense		**Perfect Tense**	
audi-am	I shall / will hear	audīv-ī	I have heard
audi-ēs	etc.	audīv-istī	etc.
audi-et		audīv-it	
audi-ēmus		audīv-imus	
audi-ētis		audīv-istis	
audi-ent		audīv-ērunt	

Points to note with audiō
1. The present tense endings are the same as for amō and moneō except in the 3rd person plural where it goes -unt like regō instead of -nt.
2. The future and imperfect are identical to regō.
3. Verbs like audiō have principal parts which begin -iō, -īre. They often, but not always, continue -īvī (or -iī), -ītum.

The historic present

Sometimes, when we are telling a story, we introduce a present tense even though we are referring to the past. This is supposed to make the story more vivid and exciting. For example:

'The two friends entered the room and found, to their horror, that they were in complete darkness. An owl hooted. A door creaked. Suddenly a huge, slimy hand **comes** from nowhere, **picks** them both up and **carries** them off.'

The story *began* in the past tense, but when the slimy hand appeared, it went into the present. This type of present is called a *historic present* because it refers to the past. It is very common in Latin. When you meet it, you should translate it with a past tense in English.
E.g. If you see oppugnat and it is clearly referring to the past, you should normally translate it as *he attacked*.

So you really want to learn Latin...

Exercise 6. 8

Study the information on the opposite page about verbs like audiō. Write out the following tenses of the following verbs:

1. Present tense of dormiō, dormīre, dormīvī, dormītum = I sleep
2. Future tense of veniō, venīre, vēnī, ventum = I come
3. Imperfect tense of dormiō, dormīre, dormīvī, dormītum = I sleep
4. Perfect tense of veniō, venīre, vēnī, ventum = I come

Exercise 6. 9

Study the information on the opposite page about the historic present. Then translate the following sentences into English. They tell a (not very exciting) story, so decide as you go along whether any of the verbs are in the historic present and, if so, how you are going to translate them into English:

1. puella magistrum nōn audiēbat.
2. magister puellam monuit.
3. puella nōn audiēbat sed dormiēbat.
4. magister ad puellam vēnit.
5. puella surgit et ad magistrum ambulat.
6. amīcī puellam exspectant.
7. puella magistrō librum magnum dedit.
8. magister miser cadit.
9. puella amīcōs in viam dūxit.
10. magister sub mēnsā dormiēbat!

Exercise 6. 10

Translate into English, using the historic present where you feel it to be appropriate:

Romānī contrā Sabīnōs bellum gerēbant. Tarpeia Sabīnōs vīdit sed Sabīnī puellam nōn audīvērunt. Sabīnī scūta magna et <u>armillās</u> pulchrās habēbant. Tarpeia armillās amābat et clāmāvit. 'armillās vestrās amō et Sabīnōs in oppidum nostrum dūcam.' Sabīnī tamen puellam malam nōn amābant. in oppidum ambulant et puellam miseram scūtīs superant.

---

armilla, -ae, f. = bracelet

persōna nōn grāta
A persōna nōn grāta is someone who is not welcome.

Vocabulary 6

Verbs		Pronouns	
audiō, audīre, audīvī, audītum	I hear	quid?	What?
cadō, cadere, cecidī, cāsum	I fall	quis?	Who?
clāmō, -āre, -āvī, -ātum	I shout	**Adverbs**	
currō, currere, cucurrī, cursum	I run	cūr?	Why?
dormiō, dormīre, -īvī, -ītum	I sleep	-ne...?	Asks a question
dūcō, dūcere, dūxī, ductum	I lead	nōnne...?	Asks a question
gerō, gerere, gessī, gestum	I conduct, wage		(expecting 'yes')
		num...?	Asks a question
regō, regere, rēxī, rēctum	I rule		(expecting 'no')
scrībō, scrībere, scrīpsī, scrīptum	I write	ubī?	Where?
surgō, surgere, surrēxī, surrēctum	I rise	**Noun**	
terreō, -ēre, -uī, -itum	I terrify	amīcus, amīcī, m.	friend
veniō, venīre, vēnī, ventum	I come		

Verbs with yukky principal parts

We have already seen how the last two principal parts of verbs like regō follow no particular pattern and just have to be learnt. Well, this is all fine and dandy unless you come across one of these beasts and (horror of horrors) you have not learnt its principal parts. Imagine the scene. There you are, snoozing quietly at the back of the class, or trying to read what Tom or Lucy has written as the answer to question 4. The teacher approaches. His voice booms out: 'Translate magister ad terram cecidit, you horrid little beast!' Quick as a flash you go straight to the verb, having been well taught by the aforesaid teacher. Cecidit... from the verb... cecidō? cecō? cōcō? Agh! You have been caught out. You do not recognise cecid- as being the perfect stem of cadō! Off with your head! No custard for a fortnight. Write out 100 times 'I am a clot and should learn my principal parts before settling down to watch T.V.'.

But there is clearly a problem here. You have to know the principal parts of cadō to recognise cecidit. But suppose you have never met cadō at all. Then what? Easy. You look it up at the back under the form you think it comes from. You would probably start with cecidō; and lo! There in the vocabulary it has cecidī: see cadō. It's as if the vocabulary can read your mind. So you go to cadō and lo! The principal parts are cadō, cadere, CECIDĪ, cāsum. Or, for coēgit, you look up coegō and there you find cōgō, with the principal parts cōgō, cōgere, COĒGĪ, coāctum. Job done. Now, don't bother me. I'm trying to snooze.

So you really want to learn Latin...

Exercise 6. 11
Study the information on the opposite page about verbs with yukky principal parts. It is the perfect tense that normally gives the trouble, so, as a warm-up, give the Latin for:

1. We have ruled
2. They have risen
3. She has run
4. I have written
5. You (sing.) have led
6. She has destroyed
7. We have sat
8. They have feared
9. We have remained
10. He has given

Exercise 6. 12
Now for the tricky one. Most of the verbs below are ones you have not yet met. Do not panic, just follow the advice given on the opposite page and you should be fine. Translate into English:

1. coēgit
2. iēcērunt
3. mīsistis
4. cecidistī
5. iussit
6. lūsistī
7. stetit
8. scrīpsimus
9. dedit
10. gessērunt

Exercise 6. 13
But you can't just assume that all tricky-looking verbs are in the perfect tense. The present and perfect tenses are often frighteningly similar. Try the following:

1. lūdit
2. lūsit
3. mittimus
4. mīsimus
5. cōgimus
6. coēgimus
7. venit
8. vēnit
9. dūcimus
10. dūximus

Exercise 6. 14
From which Latin words do the following derive? Translate the Latin word and explain the meaning of the English one:

1. Transmit
2. Library
3. Clamour
4. Regent
5. Surge
6. Resurrection
7. Scribe
8. Audition
9. Dormitory
10. Amicable

Using Latin

extrā
The word extrā is simply the Latin word for outside. Thus, at a restaurant, service may be extra (i.e. outside the price shown on the bill).

The kings of Rome (part 1)

Romulus (753-715) ruled in Rome for 38 years. One day in 715 BC, when he was reviewing his troops on the Campus Martius, a cloud came down and he was totally enveloped. When the cloud lifted, Romulus was gone.

The Romans thought he had been taken up to heaven and worshipped him as a god, giving him the name Quirinus. After his death Rome was ruled by **Numa Pompilius (715-673)**. Numa is most famous for his building of the temple of Janus. The doors of this temple were kept open while Rome was at war and shut while she was at peace. It is a mark of Rome's warlike character that these doors were very rarely closed. Numa will also be remembered for his affair with a fortune-telling nymph called Egeria, whom the king used to meet in a secluded grotto and ask for advice.

After the death of Numa, Rome was ruled by **Tullus Hostilius (673-642)**. Tullus was very warlike and spent most of his time beating up the local tribes such as the Albani (from Alba Longa).

After the death of Tullus, **Ancus Martius (642-617)** became king. Ancus extended Roman rule from the city all the way west to the coast, where he is said to have built the port of Ostia at the mouth of the River Tiber, but almost certainly didn't! Ostia was the main port of Rome and was vital as a means of getting corn into the city when the population began to grow.

When Ancus died, the throne passed not to one of his sons but to an Etruscan called **Tarquinius Priscus (616-579)**. During the reign of Tarquinius Priscus, a rather strange thing happened. A slave boy, Tullius, was sleeping in the palace when it was noticed that flames were dancing around his head. This was taken as an omen and the boy was brought up as a prince and betrothed to the king's daughter. Everyone was very excited except for the sons of Ancus, who were furious at having been passed over for the throne again. In their rage they burst into the palace and murdered Tarquinius Priscus, hoping to seize the throne for themselves. However the slave boy, Tullius, drove them away and was proclaimed king. Because of his servile origins, he was known as **Servius Tullius (578-535)**.

N.B. These dates are taken from the Oxford Classical Dictionary, 2nd edition. They are what is called *traditional*, i.e. no one has the faintest idea really but we need to have dates so someone comes up with some and we trot off and learn them. Good system, eh?

So you really want to learn Latin...

Exercise 6. 15

Read the information on the opposite page about the kings of Rome. Then answer the following questions in complete sentences:

1. Who was the first king of Rome and what were the dates of his reign?
2. What happened to him while he was reviewing his troops on the Campus Martius?
3. What did the Romans think had happened to him?
4. What name did they give to him after his death?
5. Who succeeded Romulus and what were the dates of his reign?
6. What was he best known for?
7. What was special about the doors of the temple of Janus?
8. Who was Egeria?
9. Who became king after Numa and what were his dates?
10. What did Tullus spend most of his time doing?
11. Who ruled after Tullus and what were his dates?
12. Which port did Ancus probably not build, and where did he probably not build it?
13. What was the importance of Ostia to the city of Rome?
14. Who ruled after Ancus, and what were his dates?
15. Describe the strange incident which happened in the palace during the reign of Tarquinius Priscus.
16. What happened to the slave boy, Tullius, as a result of this incident?
17. What did the sons of Ancus do as a result of it?
18. Who became king after the murder of Tarquinius?

Using Latin

in tōtō
The Latin phrase in tōtō = in total, or in all.
For example, the job was completed in tōtō.

CHAPTER 7
The mixed conjugation; Roman numerals

Verbs like capiō

There is one more conjugation, called the mixed conjugation, which is a combination of the 3rd and 4th.

capiō, capere, cēpī, captum = I capture, I take

Present Tense
capi-ō	I capture
cap-is	You capture
cap-it	He, she, it captures
cap-imus	We capture
cap-itis	You capture
capi-unt	They capture

Imperfect Tense
capi-ēbam	I was capturing
capi-ēbās	etc.
capi-ēbat	
capi-ēbāmus	
capi-ēbātis	
capi-ēbant	

Future Tense
capi-am	I shall / will capture
capi-ēs	etc.
capi-et	
capi-ēmus	
capi-ētis	
capi-ent	

Perfect Tense
cēp-ī	I have captured
cēp-istī	etc.
cēp-it	
cēp-imus	
cēp-istis	
cēp-ērunt	

Mixed conjugation verbs go like capiō.
1. Although they start -iō (like audiō), their 2nd principal part goes -ere (like regō).
2. Their endings are exactly like audio **when this leads to two vowels together** (e.g. capiō, capiunt, capiam, etc.), and like regō when this is not the case (e.g. capis, capit, capimus, etc.).
3. For the time being (apart from the present infinitive in -ere) this only affects the pronunciation of the i in the present tense, so treat capiō like audiō and you will be fine.

Breaking up inverted commas: inquit / inquiunt

Sometimes a speech in inverted commas is interrupted by a phrase such as *he said, he asked*, etc. In Latin this will normally be inquit = he / she says / said or inquiunt = they say / they said. The use of other verbs (e.g. rogō, clāmō, dīcō) is best avoided with direct speech in this way. Even if the English says, for example, *he asked*, use inquit if you are quoting the direct speech.

When speech is broken up in this way, just crack on as if nothing had happened, translating everything in the inverted commas as one clause or sentence, and then putting the *he said* bit where you want. If the direct speech is a question, you should obviously translate inquit as *he asked* rather than *he said*.
E.g. 'nōnne ad oppidum' inquit puer 'ambulāvistī?' = 'Have you walked to the town?' asked the boy.

So you really want to learn Latin...

Exercise 7. 1

Study the information on the opposite page about verbs like capiō. Note how they can be recognised by the fact that, although their 1st principal part goes -iō (like audiō), their 2nd principal part goes -ere (like regō). Write out the following:

1. Present tense of cupiō, cupere, cupīvī, cupītum = I want, desire
2. Future tense of fugiō, fugere, fūgī, fugitum = I flee
3. Imperfect tense of faciō, facere, fēcī, factum = I do, make

Exercise 7. 2

Read the information on the opposite page about breaking up inverted commas with inquit / inquiunt. Then translate into English:

1. 'quis' inquit puer 'meum librum cēpit?'
2. 'īnsulam magnam' inquiunt nautae 'capere cupimus!'
3. 'Mārce!' magister inquit. 'cūr nōn festīnābās?'
4. 'quis' inquit puella 'Mārcum ad agrōs dūcet?'

Exercise 7. 3

Translate into Latin, using inquit or inquiunt where appropriate. Notice how inquit / inquiunt tend to come after the first word or two of the Latin, rather than coming at the end as in English.

1. A small girl was sailing towards Italy.
2. She wanted to flee out of the town.
3. 'What are you doing?' asked a sailor.
4. 'I want to come to Italy,' the girl said.
5. At last the sailor led the girl towards a town.
6. She came towards the wretched inhabitants.
7. 'Why have you come?' the wretched inhabitants asked.
8. 'I want to live near your beautiful town,' she said.

Exercise 7. 4

Translate into English:

post cēnam, puellae agricolīs cantābant. fīlius dominī puellās audīre cupiēbat. 'cūr' inquit 'puellae cantant?' 'Mārce,' inquit dominus, 'puellae dē silvīs Ītaliae cantant.' 'quid facient' inquit Mārcus 'post cēnam?' 'puerōs' inquit dominus 'puellae vītābunt et servī puerōs in viās pellent!'

tempus fugit
This phrase is often seen on clocks and sun-dials.
In Latin tempus fugit = time flies.

Roman numerals

The numerals we use are Arabic numerals (1, 2, 3 etc.). The Romans, as you would expect, used Roman numerals (I, II, III, etc.) Numerals, when written as *words*, may be cardinal (one, two, three, etc.) or ordinal (first, second, third, etc.). The numerals from 1-10 are as follows:

Numerals	Cardinals	Ordinals
I	ūnus	prīmus
II	duŏ	secundus
III	trēs	tertius
IV/IIII	quattuor	quārtus
V	quīnque	quīntus
VI	sex	sextus
VII	septem	septimus
VIII	octŏ	octāvus
IX	novem	nōnus
X	decem	decimus

Of the numerals, only ūnus, duŏ and trēs decline (you will learn how later). Ordinals decline like bonus and must agree with the noun they describe.
E.g. the first boy = puer prīmus; the first girl = puella prīma; etc.

Numerals 11-1000!

Luckily you won't often have to translate the Latin for three hundred and seventy two, because large numbers tend to be written as numerals rather than as words. But you should be able to count up to 100 and to read and write larger numbers using Roman numerals, so here they are:

11	XI	ūndecim	30	XXX	trīgintā
12	XII	duodecim	40	XL	quadrāgintā
13	XIII	tredecim	50	L	quīnquāgintā
14	XIV	quattuordecim	60	LX	sexāgintā
15	XV	quīndecim	70	LXX	septuāgintā
16	XVI	sēdecim	80	LXXX	octōgintā
17	XVII	septendecim	90	XC	nōnāgintā
18	XVIII	duodēvīgintī	100	C	centum
19	XIX	ūndēvīgintī	500	D	quīngentī
20	XX	vīgintī	1000	M	mīlle

Using these numerals you can write any number up to 1000. Build the number up in blocks (hundreds, tens, units).
E.g.   357 = 300+50+7 = CCC+L+VII = CCCLVII
        879 = 800+70+9 = DCCC+LXX+IX = DCCCLXXIX

So you really want to learn Latin...

Exercise 7. 5
Study the information on the opposite page about Roman numerals. Then give the Latin for:

1. One boy; the first boy
2. Two farmers; the second farmer
3. Three sailors; the third sailor
4. Four girls; the fourth girl
5. Five women; the fifth woman
6. Six years; the sixth year
7. Seven Romans; the seventh Roman
8. Eight arrows; the eighth arrow
9. Nine spears: the ninth spear
10. Ten islands; the tenth island
11. Eleven masters; twenty masters
12. Twelve tables; one hundred tables

Exercise 7. 6
Write in Roman numerals:

1. 7
2. 11
3. 30
4. 44
5. 88
6. 150
7. 300
8. 845
9. 900
10. 1000

Exercise 7. 7
Write in Arabic numerals. Some of the answers are bigger than 1000, but I'm sure you will cope.

1. XLV
2. CCLIV
3. DCCLIII
4. MLXVI
5. LII
6. XLI
7. LXI
8. LXXXIX
9. MM
10. MCMXCIX

Exercise 7. 8
From which Latin words do the following derive? Translate the Latin word and explain the meaning of the English one, showing the connection between the English and Latin. It may help to know that the Roman year began in March.

1. Octet
2. Quintuplets
3. Duet
4. November
5. Tertiary
6. Quartet
7. Secondary
8. Century
9. Millennium
10. December

tandem
A tandem is a long bicycle. The name is a pun on the Latin word tandem = at length.

fīlius, deus, vir

The following nouns are 2nd declension but have some slightly strange forms. Strange forms are shown in bold, just in case you didn't spot them.

Nom.	fīlius = son	deus = god	**vir** = man (as opposed to woman)
Voc.	**fīlī**	**deus**	**vir**
Acc.	fīlium	deum	virum
Gen.	**fīlī** (or fīliī)	deī	virī
Dat.	fīliō	deō	virō
Abl.	fīliō	deō	virō
Nom.	fīliī	**dī** (or deī)	virī
Voc.	fīliī	**dī** (or deī)	virī
Acc.	fīliōs	deōs	virōs
Gen.	fīliōrum	deōrum (or **deum**)	virōrum (or **virum**)
Dat.	fīliīs	**dīs** (or deīs)	virīs
Abl.	fīliīs	**dīs** (or deīs)	virīs

Both fīlius and deus have 1st declension feminine versions (fīlia = daughter and dea = goddess). These decline like mēnsa but, to avoid confusion in the dative and ablative plural, they go fīliābus and deābus.

Vocabulary 7

Verbs

aperiō, -īre, aperuī, apertum	I open	equus, equī, m.	horse
capiō, -ere, cēpī, captum	I capture, take	fīlia, -ae, f.	daughter
cupiō, -ere, cupīvī, cupītum	I want, desire	fīlius, fīlī (fīliī), m.	son
errō, -āre, -āvī, -ātum	I wander, err	gladius, gladiī, m.	sword
faciō, -ere, fēcī, factum	I do, make	mūrus, mūrī, m.	wall
inquit / inquiunt	he says / they say	oppidum, oppidī, n.	town
pellō, -ere, pepulī, pulsum	I drive	silva, -ae, f.	wood, forest
servō, -āre, -āvī, -ātum	I save	vir, virī, m.	man
vītō -āre, -āvī, -ātum	I avoid	**Adjectives**	
Nouns		novus, -a, -um	new
cēna, -ae, f.	dinner	parvus, -a, -um	small
dea, -ae, f.	goddess	**Adverb**	
deus, deī, m.	god	tandem	at length

Revision

Check that you know by heart:
- amō, moneō, regō and audiō in 4 tenses
- capiō
- mēnsa, annus, bellum, puer and magister
- bonus
- tener and pulcher
- cardinals 1-20
- ordinals 1st-10th
- Vocabularies 1-7

So you really want to learn Latin...

Exercise 7. 9

Study the information on the opposite page about fīlius, deus and vir. Note the strange forms for fīlia and dea in the dative and ablative plural. Then translate into Latin:

1. The son of the god ruled the Romans.
2. The Romans used to sing to the gods.
3. The men gave gifts to the goddesses.
4. The good man gave a horse to the sons and daughters.
5. The gods warned the inhabitants of Troy about the war.

Exercise 7. 10

Translate into English:

1. fīlius parvus virī ad oppidum novum festīnāvit.
2. agricolās vītāvit et equum ad fīliam deae dūxit.
3. puella dīs prope mūrōs oppidī cantābat.
4. puer per viās oppidī errābat.
5. tandem ex oppidō vēnit et īn* silvās festīnāvit.

   N.B. In Latin, a vowel is always long when followed by ns or nf. Note that this applies to the word in when it comes before a word beginning with s or f.

Exercise 7. 11

Study the words in Vocabulary 7. From which Latin words do the following derive? Translate the Latin word and explain the meaning of the English one.

1. Error
2. Novelty
3. Captive
4. Equine
5. Mural
6. Virile
7. Aperture
8. Repel
9. Fact
10. Audition

Exercise 7. 12

Look at the points for revision on the opposite page. Make sure that you know all of this by heart. You should be able to write out all of the grammar from memory, and must know your vocabulary *both ways* (i.e. English into Latin as well as Latin into English). Make a list of the words you are not sure of. To help you learn them, try to think of at least one English derivation for each one.

Using Latin

īn sitū
The Latin phrase īn sitū means in position.
For example: 'They decided to mend it īn sitū.'

The kings of Rome (part 2)

So there he was, a mere slave, king of Rome. Servius Tullius, the boy whose head had caught fire in the palace without so much as a hair being harmed, king. The trouble was, though, everybody called him Servius, because they all knew he was really only a slave.

So the new king took steps to improve his street credibility. He began by marrying his daughters off to the sons of the murdered king. One daughter, an ambitious and somewhat violent girl called Tullia, was married off to the mild and gentle Arruns Tarquinius. Her sister, mild and gentle (and also called Tullia), was married to the hot-headed and super-ambitious Lucius Tarquinius. The marriages were, of course, a complete disaster, and it was not long before the ambitious pair had disposed of their mild and gentle partners and had married each other.

Lucius Tarquinius soon had ambitions on the throne and, encouraged by his wife, rushed into the senate-house, sat in the king's chair, and began laying into the king for being a mere slave. When Servius Tullius arrived and found his son-in-law in his chair, he was not pleased, but Lucius Tarquinius picked the old king up, dragged him from the senate-house and hurled him down the steps into the forum. The king's supporters fled and, as the old king made his way slowly home, Lucius Tarquinius's men knifed him and left him dying in the street. Meanwhile the odious Tullia was parading around the forum, hailing her husband as king. She then climbed into her carriage and set off for the palace. On the way she passed the body of her dead father. Far from stopping, she ordered her driver to drive over the body and was splashed with her father's blood. The spot was known ever afterwards as the Street of Crime and can be seen in Rome to this day.

As for Lucius Tarquinius, he was to rule from 534 until 510. He began his reign by refusing to allow the body of the old king to be buried. He then killed a large number of the aristocracy, or patricians, so that there would be less of them to complain about his oppressive rule. Admittedly he conquered many neighbouring tribes and was a very successful general but the people hated him and he was soon given the nickname Tarquinius Superbus (Tarquin the Proud). The final straw came when his son raped a girl called Lucretia. The girl's husband was away with the army at the time but she immediately sent for him and the rest of her family to tell them what had happened. Then, having made them promise to seek revenge on the odious house of Tarquin, she killed herself, unable to bear the shame of what had happened.

Thus it was that, urged on by a friend called Lucius Junius Brutus, the family of Lucretia drove the hated Tarquins from Rome. What is more, the people of Rome were determined that they should not again suffer at the hands of a wicked king and from 510 B.C. Rome was ruled as a republic. Supreme power lay with two consuls who held office for one year, and who were chosen from and were answerable to the senate, a sort of parliament made up of members of the patrician class. Never again were kings to rule in that city. Indeed when Julius Caesar, hundreds of years later, began swaggering about as if he were a king, he got knifed. But that's another story.

So you really want to learn Latin...

Exercise 7.13

Read the information on the opposite page about the kings of Rome. Then answer the following questions in complete sentences:

1. Why was Servius Tullius called Servius?
2. What steps did Servius take to improve his street credibility?
3. Explain why the marriages of Servius's two daughters were not successful.
4. Who was Lucius Tarquinius? Draw a simple family tree to show the relationship between Lucius Tarquinius, Tarquinius Priscus, Servius Tullius, and the two Tullia daughters.
5. Describe what happened when Lucius Tarquinius rushed into the Senate house and sat in the king's chair.
6. What happened to Servius Tullius as he made his way home?
7. What did Tullia do as she made her way home?
8. Where did this unpleasant family scene take place?
9. Give the dates of Lucius Tarquinius as king of Rome.
10. Explain how he acquired the name Superbus.
11. How did the rape of Lucretia lead to the expulsion of the family of the Tarquins?
12. Describe how Rome was ruled after 510 B.C.

Using Latin

pater noster
The Lord's Prayer is sometimes referred to as the pater noster. In Latin, pater noster = our father.

CHAPTER 8

3rd declension nouns; more on adjectives; apposition

3rd declension nouns: rēx and opus

Nouns of the 3rd declension have a genitive singular ending in -is and decline like rēx:

	rēx, rēg-is, m. = king	
Nom.	rēx	rēg-ēs
Voc.	rēx	rēg-ēs
Acc.	rēg-em	rēg-ēs
Gen.	rēg-is	rēg-um
Dat.	rēg-ī	rēg-ibus
Abl.	rēg-e	rēg-ibus

Masculine and feminine nouns decline like rēx. Neuter nouns behave as you would expect. Thus opus:

	opus, oper-is, n. = work	
Nom.	opus	oper-a
Voc.	opus	oper-a
Acc.	opus	oper-a
Gen.	oper-is	oper-um
Dat.	oper-ī	oper-ibus
Abl.	oper-e	oper-ibus

Working with 3rd declension nouns

The secret to success when using 3rd declension nouns is getting the stem right. You should be used to working with stems by now, but in the 3rd declension there is often a dramatic and totally unpredictable change in the stem. Thus, whereas mēnsa has the perfectly reasonable stem of mēns-, and annus has the stem ann-, the 3rd declension noun rēx has a stem of rēg-, and opus has a stem of oper-. And if you think that's bad, take a look at iūdex, which has the stem iūdic-, or mīles, which has the stem mīlit-. Pretty weird, eh?

Another thing to look out for is that neuter nouns in -us look rather as if they should go like annus. The genitive singular however should make it clear that they are 3rd declension.

Common nouns

You have already come across the idea of nouns being common, i.e. they can be either masculine or feminine. 3rd declension nouns which are common decline just like a masculine or feminine one would, i.e. like rēx.

So you really want to learn Latin...

Exercise 8. 1

Study the information on the opposite page about 3rd declension nouns like rēx. Notice how, once you have got past the vocative singular, the endings are added to the stem (which is found, as usual, in the genitive singular). Note also the information on *common* nouns. Write out in full:

1. mīles, mīlit-is, c. = soldier
2. cōnsul, cōnsul-is, m. = consul
3. dux, duc-is, c. = leader

Exercise 8. 2

Translate the following into Latin:

1. The kings were ruling in the city.
2. The soldiers were waging many wars.
3. We will attack the city with many arrows.
4. Why has the leader warned the soldiers?
5. The Romans captured the leader of the city.

Exercise 8. 3

Notice how extra care needs to be taken when translating sentences with 3rd declension nouns, because the nominative and accusative plural endings are the same. Follow the rules of translation carefully (VERB FIRST!) and you will cruise through these. Now translate into English:

1. rēx Rōmānōrum mīlitēs monuit.
2. mīlitēs ducem ad urbem dūxērunt.
3. Rōmulus urbem magnam aedificāvit.
4. mīlitēs urbem oppugnāvērunt.
5. mīlitēs prope urbem superāvimus.

Exercise 8. 4

Study the information on the opposite page about 3rd declension neuter nouns like opus. Notice how, once you have got past the nominative, vocative and accusative singular, the endings are added to the stem (which is found in the genitive singular). Write out in full:

1. flūmen, flūmin-is, n. = river
2. carmen, carmin-is, n. = poem, song
3. nōmen, nōmin-is, n. = name

Using Latin

opus

opus = 'work' is often used to refer to the works of musical composers. E.g. Beethoven's Ninth Symphony, Opus 125.

Agreement of adjectives with 3rd declension nouns

Care needs to be taken when making an adjective such as bonus agree with a noun such as rēx. Nothing strange happens, but you may *feel* something strange is happening because the two words stand almost no chance of rhyming. Gone are the happy days of puella bona, or dominus bonus. Now we have to put up with rēx bonus (masculine), urbs bona (feminine) and opus bonum (neuter). Don't panic! Stick to the rules of adjective agreement and you will be fine.

Adjectives and common nouns

Common nouns are those that could be either masculine or feminine. When making an adjective agree with a common noun, it is normal to assume that the noun is masculine, unless there is some good reason to make it feminine.

Vocabulary 8

Nouns				
arbor, arbŏris, f.	tree	pater, patris, m.	father
carmen carminis, n.	song	pōns, pontis, m.	bridge
cōnsul, cōnsulis, m.	consul	rēx, rēgis, m.	king
cubīle, cubīlis, n.	bed	urbs, urbis, f.	city
dux, ducis, c.	leader	**Adjectives**	
flūmen, flūminis, n.	river	altus, -a, -um	high, deep
frāter, frātris, m.	brother	superbus, -a, -um	proud
hostis*, hostis, c.	enemy	**Verbs**	
māter, mātris, f.	mother	appellō, -āre, -āvī, -ātum	I call
mīles, mīlitis, c.	soldier	frangō, -ere, frēgī, frāctum	I break
nōmen, nōminis, n.	name	**Adverbs**	
opus, operis, n.	work	diū	for a long time
		ōlim	once upon a time

* hostis is generally used in the plural unless referring specifically to one single enemy.
E.g. hostēs spectābat. = He was watching the enemy.

Apposition

When we say something like 'I led Julia, my friend, into the street' we are using apposition. The words 'my friend' are in *apposition* to 'Julia,' because they explain or describe her and **must go in the same case** as she does.
E.g. Iūliam, amīcam meam, in viam dūcēbam. = I led Julia, my friend, into the street.
E.g. Mārcus, amīcus meus, in viam festīnāvit. = Marcus, my friend, hurried into the street.
E.g. māter Mārcī, puerī bonī, in viam festīnāvit. = The mother of Marcus, a good boy, hurried into the street.

nōmine = by name

The best way of translating the English word *called* (as in 'a boy called Marcus') is to use the ablative singular of nōmen = name.
E.g. The boy called Marcus = puer nōmine Mārcus (i.e. the boy *by name* Marcus).

So you really want to learn Latin...

Exercise 8. 5

Study the information on the opposite page about the agreement of adjectives with 3rd declension and *common* nouns. Remember, adjective agreement has nothing to do with rhyming. When it rhymes, it's a fluke. After all, agricol**a** bon**us** didn't rhyme, and we coped with that. So, just work out which case and gender the noun is and then put the adjective into that form.

1. The good kings (nom.)
2. O bad king!
3. The tired soldier (acc.)
4. Of the small river
5. For the new work
6. Without a good leader
7. Towards the big city
8. Under the small bridge
9. With our soldiers
10. Of the angry leader

Exercise 8. 6

Translate into English:

1. in flūmen altum
2. in flūmine altō
3. prope pontem magnum
4. contrā mīlitēs fessōs
5. cum rēge malō
6. dē arbore magnā
7. ante carmen pulchrum
8. sine nōmine
9. post mortem
10. circum urbem magnam

Exercise 8. 7

Study the information on the opposite page about apposition and the use of nōmine = by name. Then translate into English:

1. rēx malus, nōmine Tarquinius, Rōmānōs diū terrēbat.
2. puella, nōmine Lucrētia, fīlium rēgis superbī timēbat.
3. mīlitēs Brūtī Tarquinium ex urbe pellēbant.
4. Tarquinius Superbus auxilium ā rēge, nōmine Porsennā, cupiēbat.
5. 'num' inquit Brūtus 'urbem nostram servābimus?'
6. 'hostēs' inquit Horātius 'superābō et pontem frangētis.'

Exercise 8. 8

Translate into English:

ōlim rēx, nōmine Tarquinius Superbus, Rōmānōs terrēbat. fīlius rēgis, Sextus Tarquinius, puellam pulchram amāvit. puella puerum timēbat et clāmāvit. amīcī, tamen, nōn audīvērunt. tandem mīles īrātus, nōmine Brūtus, rēgem superbum superāvit et ex urbe pepulit. Rōmānī miserī rēgēs nōn cupiēbant et diū <u>duōs</u> cōnsulēs habēbant. <u>alter</u> mīlitēs dūcēbat, <u>alter</u> urbem regēbat.

---

duōs = acc. pl. of duŏ = two; alter...alter = one (of two)...the other (of two).

Using Latin

post mortem
A post mortem (= after death) examination is carried out on a body after death.

Non-increasing 3rd declension nouns: cīvis and cubīle

Most 3rd declension nouns have one more syllable in their genitive singular than in their nominative singular, and are thus said to be *increasing*.

E.g. rēx (1 syllable); rēgis (2 syllables)
    mīles (2 syllables); mīlitis (3 syllables)
    tempestās (3 syllables); tempestātis (4 syllables)

But there is a class of 3rd declension nouns which does not behave like this and is thus called *non-increasing*.

E.g. cīvis (2 syllables); cīvis (2 syllables)
    cubīle (3 syllables); cubīlis (3 syllables)

Masculine and feminine non-increasing nouns decline like cīvis, cīvis, c. = citizen. Neuter ones decline like cubīle, cubīlis, n. = bed. The endings to watch out for are shown in bold.

Nom.	cīvis	cubīle
Voc.	cīvis	cubīle
Acc.	cīv-**em**	cubīle
Gen.	cīv-is	cubīl-is
Dat.	cīv-ī	cubīl-ī
Abl.	cīv-e	cubīl-**ī**
Nom.	cīv-**ēs**	cubīl-**ia**
Voc.	cīv-**ēs**	cubīl-**ia**
Acc.	cīv-**ēs**	cubīl-**ia**
Gen.	cīv-**ium**	cubīl-**ium**
Dat.	cīv-ibus	cubīl-ibus
Abl.	cīv-ibus	cubīl-ibus

Common exceptions

There are some nouns which *increase* but which take their endings from cīvis and cubīle, and there are some which do *not* increase, but which take their endings from rēx and opus.

1. The following non-increasing nouns go like rēx (i.e. they go -um in the genitive plural): senex (old man), iuvenis (young man), pater (father), māter (mother), frāter (brother), soror (sister), canis (dog). These are easy to remember because they are all members of the family – even the dog is there!

2. Monosyllables which have a stem ending in two consonants go like cīvis (i.e. they go -ium in the genitive plural):
E.g. urbs, urb-is, f. = city; fōns, font-is, m = fountain; mōns, mont-is, m. = mountain.

3. Increasing *neuter* nouns ending in -al or -ar go like cubīle.
E.g. animal, animālis, n. = animal (nom. pl. = animālia etc.).

So you really want to learn Latin...

Exercise 8. 9
Study the information on the opposite page about increasing and non-increasing nouns. Note the basic rule and the common exceptions. Now write out in full:
1. hostis, hostis, c. = enemy
2. animal, animālis, n. = animal
3. pōns, pontis, m. = bridge
4. frāter, frātris, m. = brother
5. urbs, urbis, f. = city

Exercise 8. 10
Translate into Latin:
1. The enemy prepared the bridges and gates of the city.
2. The Romans watched the enemy from the city.
3. They attacked the city with many arrows and spears.
4. The leader of the enemy ran across the bridge.
5. The Romans killed the soldier and dragged the body into the city.

Exercise 8. 11
Translate into Latin, remembering to use inquit / inquiunt when quoting direct speech:

Tarquin the Proud was attacking Rome. He was leading his forces towards the city. A Roman soldier, called Horatius, hurried across the bridge. 'What are you doing?' asked the Romans. 'I will save our city,' said Horatius. 'I will fight with the enemy and you will break the bridge.'

Exercise 8. 12
From which Latin words do the following derive? Translate the Latin word and explain the meaning of the English one.

1. Civilian
2. Urban
3. Superb
4. Altitude
5. Hostile
6. Arboretum
7. Maternal
8. Paternal
9. Juvenile
10. Canine

Using Latin

in locō parentis
in locō parentis = in the place of a parent.

Horatius holds the bridge

Tarquin the Proud was not especially pleased to have been booted out of Rome and sought help from Lars Porsenna, king of Clusium, who marched on Rome at the head of a huge army of hairy Etruscans. He captured the Janiculum hill and was preparing to cross the River Tiber at the Pons Sublicius. But it was here that a seriously brave Roman called Horatius Cocles took up his station, determined to save the city. He realised that the only way to frustrate the enemy was to destroy the bridge before they could cross. So, calling for assistance from two companions, Spurius Lartius and Titus Herminius, he marched across to the far side of the bridge and held off the Etruscan army, while the rest of the Romans began to hack away at the bridge.

As soon as the bridge had become seriously creaky and was about to collapse, Horatius sent his two companions back to safety while he himself continued to hold off the enemy single-handed.

Suddenly there was an almighty crash and a couple of tons of Pons Sublicius fell into the Tiber and headed for the sea. Horatius had saved Rome. However the hairy Etruscans were in no mood for handing out congratulations and Horatius realised that it was time to make a swift exit. Holding his arms up in prayer the young man called upon the river god, Father Tiber, with the words 'accept this man and these arms into your waters.' He then leapt, fully armed, into the river and swam to safety on the other side.

So you really want to learn Latin...

Exercise 8. 13

Read the story of Horatius holding the bridge on the opposite page and then answer the following questions in complete sentences:

1. Why was Tarquinius Superbus not pleased?
2. From whom did he seek help?
3. What success did Lars Porsenna have in his attempt to capture Rome?
4. At which bridge over the Tiber were the Etruscans held up?
5. Who resolved to prevent the enemy from crossing the bridge?
6. Who were his two companions?
7. What happened when the bridge was on the point of collapse?
8. What happened to Horatius when the bridge finally did collapse?
9. Why do you think Roman fathers used to tell this story to their children?
10. Which stories of bravery might we use today?

Using Latin

ab initiō
The Latin phrase ab initiō = from the beginning.
For example: 'Let us begin ab initiō.'

CHAPTER 9
Linking sentences and clauses; revision

 Linking sentences and clauses

Sentences and clauses are joined together using conjunctions. So far we have struggled along using et and sed, but the time has come to wheel in some more sophisticated conjunctions.

1. **autem**
   autem = moreover or however, is used to join two sentences and is placed *second* (never first) word in the sentence. It is not a very strong word, and sometimes need not be translated into English at all.
   E.g. Rōmānī oppugnāvērunt. dux **autem** hostium cōpiās ad flūmen dūxit.
   = The Romans attacked. The leader of the enemy, (**however**), led his forces towards the river.

2. **tamen**
   tamen = however, is a much stronger word than autem and should always be translated. It, too, comes second word in the clause.
   E.g. The Romans attacked. **However** the enemy overcame the wretched soldiers. =
   Rōmānī oppugnāvērunt. hostēs **tamen** mīlitēs miserōs superāvērunt.

3. **enim**
   A clause which explains a preceding clause is often linked to it by enim = for. It is always written second (never first) word in the clause.
   E.g. The Romans attacked. **For** they wished to capture the camp. =
   Rōmānī oppugnāvērunt. castra **enim** capere cupiēbant.

4. **-que**
   (a) Nouns may be joined by **-que** = and. The -que is joined on to the end of the second noun.
   E.g. The boys **and** girls were running = puerī puellae**que** currēbant.
   (b) Clauses, too, may be joined using -que.
   E.g. The farmers were singing **and** preparing the tables. =
   agricolae cantābant mēnsās**que** parābant.
   Note how the -que is joined to the *end of the first Latin word* in the new clause. It is sometimes helpful, when translating, to substitute et for -que to make things clearer.
   E.g. agricolae cantābant mēnsās**que** parābant. =
   agricolae cantābant **et** mēnsās parābant.

So you really want to learn Latin...

Exercise 9. 1

Study paragraphs 1-4 on the opposite page about autem, tamen, enim and -que. It all looks rather scary but hey, you're in Chapter 9, you can do anything! Now translate into English:

1. quīnque puellae et quattuor puerī per viās ambulābant. pontem autem vīdērunt.
2. puellae aquam timēbant neque prope flūmen lūdēbant. Flāvia tamen in aquam cecidit.
3. agricola īrātus, nōmine Sextus, ad flūmen festīnāvit. puellam enim servāre cupiēbat.
4. puerī puellaeque aquam spectābant. Flāviam tamen non vīdērunt.
5. tandem tamen frāter puellae in flūmen dēscendit Flāviamque servāvit. puer enim Flāviam amāvit.

Exercise 9. 2

Translate into Latin:

1. The mother of the consul remained near the city. The son, however, departed.
2. The king led his soldiers towards the river. For he wanted to carry water to the camp.
3. The daughter of the king was hiding Romulus and Remus. However, the soldiers threw the boys into the river.
4. Romulus killed Remus and built the city near the river.
5. The Romans destroyed the bridge and hurried towards the city.

Exercise 9. 3

Translate into English:

ōlim in Ītaliā habitābat mōnstrum magnum nōmine Cācus. per agrōs autem errābat et agricolās terrēbat. incolae Ītaliae mōnstrum timēbant. mōnstrum enim flammās spīrābat et oculōs saevōs habēbat. tandem vir validus, nōmine Herculēs, in Ītaliam vēnit. multōs taurōs habēbat. ubĭ Cācus taurōs vīdit in spēluncam caudīs trāxit. Herculēs vestīgia taurōrum invēnit. tauros tamen nōn invēnit. animālia enim retrō ambulābant.

subitō ūnus ē taurīs clāmāvit. Herculēs ad locum festīnāvit mōnstrumque tēlō vulnerāvit. Cācum necāvit taurōsque recēpit. ita incolās perīculō servāvit.

---

flamma, -ae, f. = flame; spīrō, -āre, -āvī, -ātum = I breathe; saevus, -a, um = fierce; taurus, -ī, m. = bull; spēlunca, -ae, f. = cave; cauda, -ae, f. = tail; vestīgium, -iī, n. = track, trace; retrō = backwards; recipiō, -ere, recēpī, receptum = I take back; ita = thus.

Using Latin

forum
A forum is an opportunity for discussion. The forum in a Roman town was the main meeting and market place.

And...not

The Latin for 'and' when it is followed by 'not' is neque or nec. Never, never, never be tempted to use et followed by the normal word for 'not'.

E.g. He sleeps **and** does **not** work. = dormit **neque** labōrat.

But...not

A similar principle applies to 'but' when it is followed by 'not'. This one is not quite so rigid, but if you want to be absolutely correct in your use of Latin (which of course you do) the Latin for 'but' when it is followed by 'not' should be neque tamen or nec tamen.

E.g. He fights **but** does **not** conquer. = pugnat **nec tamen** superat.

nec...nec and et...et

1. The Latin for 'neither...nor' is nec...nec or neque...neque.
   E.g. **Neither** the sailors **nor** the farmers loved the king. =
   nec nautae **nec** agricolae rēgem amābant.

2. The Latin for 'both...and' is et...et or -que...-que
   E.g. **Both** the sailors **and** the farmers loved the king. =
   et nautae **et** agricolae rēgem amābant
   or nautae**que** agricolae**que** rēgem amābant.

Vocabulary 9

Verbs

ascendō, -ere, ascendī, ascēnsum	I go up, climb		
cōgō, cōgere, coēgī, coāctum	I force, compel		
cōnstituō, cōnstituere, cōnstituī, cōnstitūtum	I decide		
dīcō, dīcere, dīxī, dictum	I say		
discēdō, -ere, discessī, discessum	I depart		
fugiō, fugere, fūgī, fugitum	I flee		
iaciō, iacere, iēcī, iactum	I throw		
mittō, mittere, mīsī, missum	I send		
videō, vidēre, vīdī, vīsum	I see		

Adverbs

crās	tomorrow
saepe	often

Conjunctions

autem	however, moreover
dum	while
enim	for
et...et	both...and
nec/neque	and...not
nec...nec	neither...nor
neque...neque	neither...nor
nec tamen	but...not
neque tamen	but...not
tamen	however
ubĭ	when, where

Nouns

arma, -ōrum, n. pl.	weapons
corpus, corpŏris, n.	body

Adjective

barbarus, -a, -um	barbarian

So you really want to learn Latin...

Exercise 9. 4

Study the information on the opposite page about 'and not' and 'but not'. Translate into English:

1. rēx superbus Rōmānōs terrēbat neque urbem amābat.
2. pater puerōs amābat nec tamen Mārcum docēre cupiēbat.
3. puella magistrum vulnerāvit neque tamen superāvit.
4. dux hostium Rōmānōs timēbat neque mīlitēs in Ītaliam dūcēbat.
5. incolae nautās vidēbant nec tamen superābant.

Exercise 9. 5

Study the information on the opposite page about nec...nec and et...et. Then translate into Latin:

1. Both the Romans and the barbarians decided to fight.
2. Neither the boys nor the girls wanted to climb the mountain.
3. Tomorrow you will see both mountains and rivers.
4. Neither the gods nor the goddesses loved proud men.
5. When the sons of the consul entered the forum they neither listened nor watched.

Exercise 9. 6

Study the words in Vocabulary 9. Translate and then list as many derivations, English, French, Spanish and Italian, as you can for each of the following Latin words:

1. dīcunt
2. ascendēmus
3. corporis
4. fugiēbās
5. cōnstituere
6. crās
7. barbarōrum
8. arma
9. mittent
10. iēcit

Exercise 9. 7

Translate into English:

ōlim rēx, nōmine Mīnōs, īnsulam Crētam regēbat. rēx autem mōnstrum magnum in <u>labyrinthō</u> tenēbat. mōnstrum puellās puerōsque saepe necābat. rēx enim incolās <u>Athēnārum</u> in labyrinthum pepulit.

rēx Graecus, nōmine Aegeus, incolās Athēnārum regēbat. fīlius rēgis, nōmine Thēseus, labyrinthum intrāvit nec tamen mōnstrum timuit. mōnstrum necāvit incolāsque Athēnārum servāvit.

---

labyrinthus, -ī, m. = a labyrinth, maze; Athēnae, -ārum, f. pl. = Athens

ad nauseam
ad nauseam = to (the point of) sea-sickness.
For example: 'They went on and on ad nauseam.'

Mucius Scaevola

Horatius frustrated the efforts of Lars Porsenna by having the bridge destroyed, but Lars Porsenna did not give up that easily. He besieged Rome and after a while food began to run out in the city. It was then that a young Roman patrician, Gaius Mucius, had his cunning plan. Hiding his sword up his tunic he boldly approached the enemy camp. Sneaking past the guards he made for the king's tent, resolved to kill Lars Porsenna and put an end to the war. However, it was then that his cunning plan went horribly wrong. For sitting outside the tent, soaking up the rays, was the king's secretary. Mistaking this man for the king, Gaius Mucius leapt on top of him and slit his throat. A hundred million guards immediately appeared and dragged the intrepid, if somewhat startled, Roman before the real king.

When questioned as to his identity and his intentions, Gaius said that he was a Roman who had come to kill the king. 'I am a Roman citizen,' he said, 'and Roman citizens do not fear death. Nor am I alone in wanting to kill you. There are many more Roman citizens prepared to risk their lives to kill you. You will have to fight each one in turn.'

Lars Porsenna was not sure that he liked Gaius's tone, and told him so. 'I do not like your tone,' he said, 'and I may have to throw you into the fire.' But Gaius scornfully thrust his right hand into the flames with the words 'I do not fear pain.' Lars Porsenna was quite impressed by this display and sent Gaius back to Rome. Shortly afterwards he made a truce with the Romans. As for Gaius, he was rewarded with a piece of land and, following his little trick with the bonfire, came to be known as Scaevola (i.e. left-handed)!

So you really want to learn Latin...

Exercise 9. 8

Read the story of Mucius Scaevola on the opposite page and then answer the following questions in complete sentences:

1. What did Lars Porsenna do once the bridge had been destroyed and what effect did this have on the inhabitants of Rome?
2. Who was Gaius Mucius and what did he plan to do?
3. How did his plan go horribly wrong?
4. How did Gaius react when questioned by the king?
5. How did the king respond to Gaius's challenge?
6. How did Gaius show that he was not afraid of the king's threats?
7. What effect did this have on Lars Porsenna?
8. Explain how Gaius Mucius came to be known as 'Scaevola'.

Revision

It's really quite scary how much you have learnt now. Do you remember how you used to muddle your subjects and objects? So just check that you are totally happy with the following before we throw you screaming and kicking into the last chapter:

- All verbs in the four tenses
- Nouns like: mēnsa, annus, bellum, puer, magister, rēx, opus, cīvis and cubīle
- Irregular nouns: fīlius, deus and vir
- bonus, tener and pulcher
- Cardinals 1-20 and ordinals 1st-10th
- Vocabularies 1-9

Exercise 9. 9

Revision. Look above at what you are supposed to know and then translate the following, without looking up:

1. sine fīliābus
2. dē montibus
3. habuit
4. habitāvit
5. vēnērunt
6. mānsit
7. tandem
8. tēla
9. veniēs
10. viā
11. vocābāmus
12. regētis

ad absurdum
ad absurdum = to the absurd. For example:
'He exaggerated the story ad absurdum.'

CHAPTER 10

The verb 'to be'; the future perfect and pluperfect tenses

The verb 'to be'

The verb 'to be' in Latin is irregular, as it is in most languages. Just think of a poor Martian trying to learn the verb 'to be' in English: I *am*, you *are*, he *is*... Quite a head-ache for the poor little chap!

In Latin the verb 'to be' is sum and goes as follows. For those of you who know some French, note how similar the present tense of sum is to the verb 'to be' in French. N.B. a French circumflex accent often marks where a letter 's' has dropped out (e.g. vous êtes).

sum, esse, fuī = I am

Present Tense		Imperfect Tense	
sum	I am	eram	I was
es	You (sing.) are	erās	You (sing.) were
est	He, she, it is	erat	He, she, it was
sumus	We are	erāmus	We were
estis	You (pl.) are	erātis	You (pl.) were
sunt	They are	erant	They were
Future Tense		**Perfect Tense**	
erō	I shall / will be	fuī	I have been
eris	You (sing.) will be	fuistī	You (sing.) have been
erit	He, she, it will be	fuit	He, she, it has been
erimus	We shall / will be	fuimus	We have been
eritis	You (pl.) will be	fuistis	You have been
erunt	They will be	fuērunt	They have been

sum and complements

The verb 'to be' tells us something about the subject of the sentence and is thus followed by *a complement* **in the nominative case**. The complement may be a noun or an adjective. Note how the verb 'to be' in Latin sometimes comes where it does in English, rather than at the end of the sentence:
E.g.   Marcus is tired. = Mārcus fessus est.
E.g.   Marcus was a soldier. = Mārcus erat mīles.

There is / there are

The verb 'to be' is often found in the 3rd person at the beginning of a sentence with the meaning 'there is' or 'there are':
E.g.   iam sunt duŏ cōnsulēs. = Now there are two consuls.
E.g.   ōlim erat mīles magnus. = Once there was a great soldier.

So you really want to learn Latin...

Exercise 10. 1
Study all the information on the opposite page about the verb 'to be'. Then translate into English:
1. Mūcius mīles Rōmānus est.
2. Tarquinius erat rēx superbus.
3. Aenēās fīlius deae erat.
4. iam flūmen altum est.
5. ōlim erat urbs magna, nōmine Rōma.
6. dea sapientiae erat Minerva.
7. ōlim erat fēmina pulchra.
8. nōn erimus īrātī.
9. diū nōn scrībēmus; fessī enim sumus.
10. sagittae mīlitum longae erant.

Exercise 10. 2
Study again the information on the opposite page about the verb 'to be'. Pay particular attention to what it says about the complement going in the nominative case. Then translate into Latin:
1. She is tired.
2. We are angry.
3. The farmers are proud.
4. There was a boy called Gaius.
5. You are not barbarians, are you?
6. The trees are big.
7. Where are the soldiers of the king?
8. Who is the leader of the inhabitants?
9. Tomorrow she will be tired.
10. Why is the schoolmaster angry again?

Exercise 10. 3
Study the principal parts of sum given on the opposite page. Note that sum only has three principal parts. This is not a problem, though, and the perfect tense of sum is formed from the 3rd principal part, as it is for all other verbs. Give the Latin for:
1. I have been
2. You (sing.) have been
3. He, she, it has been
4. We have been
5. You (pl.) have been
6. They have been

magnum opus
magnum opus = great work is often used to describe someone's ultimate or finest work.

To be or not to be?

Once you have met the verb 'to be', there is a danger that you will start putting it in all over the place. For example: *He is walking*. This comes from the verb 'to walk' and has nothing to do with the verb 'to be'. But you would be amazed at how many people would start off with est, for 'he is', rather than just writing ambulat as they should.

So beware. Only use the verb 'to be' when someone or something is '*being*' something. If they are *doing* something, use the appropriate verb of doing!
Thus:
 He was tired. = fessus erat.
 He was walking. = ambulābat.

The last two tenses: future perfect and pluperfect

There are two more tenses to be learnt, the endings of which will look very familiar now that you have learnt sum. The future perfect tense tells us what *will have* or *shall have* happened at some time in the future. For example, *by the end of term you will have lost your marbles*. The pluperfect tense tells us what *had* happened in the past. For example, *she had lost her marbles already*. Both of these tenses are formed by adding a set of endings to the perfect stem, found in the 3rd principal part.

Future perfect
amāv-erō	I shall have / will have loved
amāv-eris	You (sing.) will have loved
amāv-erit	He, she, it will have loved
amāv-erimus	We shall have / will have loved
amāv-eritis	You (pl.) will have loved
amāv-erint	They will have loved

Pluperfect
amāv-eram	I had loved
amāv-erās	You (sing.) had loved
amāv-erat	He, she, it had loved
amāv-erāmus	We had loved
amāv-erātis	You (pl.) had loved
amāv-erant	They had loved

Points to note

- The future perfect endings are almost identical to the future tense of sum. The one difference is the 3rd person plural goes -erint, not -erunt.
- The pluperfect tense endings are identical to the imperfect of sum.
- Verbs of *all* conjugations use these same endings, simply added to the verb's 3rd principal part.

So you really want to learn Latin...

Exercise 10. 4

Study the information on the opposite page: 'To be or not to be?'. Translate the following into Latin:

1. He is happy.
2. He is running.
3. They are tired but they are running.
4. The farmers were miserable.
5. We were watching the farmers.

Exercise 10. 5

Study the information on the opposite page about the future perfect and pluperfect tenses. Write out the following, remembering to use the perfect stem.

1. moneō in the future perfect
2. regō in the pluperfect
3. cadō in the future perfect
4. veniō in the pluperfect

Exercise 10. 6

Translate the following into English:

1. mīlitēs castra mox cēperint.
2. puellae puerōs vulnerāverant.
3. dux servōs monuerit.
4. nautae īnsulam vīderant.
5. vōcem puerī fēmina nōn audīverat.

Exercise 10. 7

Translate the following into Latin. Take care with the tense of the verbs, as they are a mixture of all the tenses you have learnt.

Gaius Mucius was a strong soldier. Roman soldiers do not fear pain. The soldier walked towards the camp of the enemy. He saw a slave near the king's table. 'I will kill the king with my sword.' The soldier had hidden a sword. 'Why have you killed the slave?' asked the king. 'The slave was not the king,' said the guards. 'Soon a Roman soldier will have killed the king,' said Mucius. 'I will come into your city,' said the king 'but I will not carry on war with the Romans.'

Using Latin

aliās
In Latin aliās = at another time. An alias is a name used at times to disguise one's true identity.

Using the principal parts

You have now learnt to use three of the verb's four principal parts. To prove that you have fully understood how Latin verbs work, you can write out a verb's principal parts as shown below, with the six tenses written out, three using the present stem and three using the perfect stem. Written out this way, dēbeō = I ought would go as follows:

dēbe-ō	**dēbē-re**	**dēbu-ī**	**dēbit-um**
dēbē-s		dēbu-istī	
dēbe-t		dēbu-it	
dēbē-mus		dēbu-imus	
dēbē-tis		dēbu-istis	
dēbe-nt		dēbu-ērunt	
dēbē-bō		**dēbu-erō**	
dēbē-bis		dēbu-eris	
dēbē-bit		dēbu-erit	
dēbē-bimus		dēbu-erimus	
dēbē-bitis		dēbu-eritis	
dēbē-bunt		dēbu-erint	
dēbē-bam		**dēbu-eram**	
dēbē-bās		dēbu-erās	
dēbē-bat		dēbu-erat	
dēbē-bāmus		dēbu-erāmus	
dēbē-bātis		dēbu-erātis	
dēbē-bant		dēbu-erant	

Vocabulary 10

Nouns

		Verbs	
caput, capitis, n.	head	agō, agere, ēgī, āctum	I do
cibus, cibī, m.	food	bibō, bibere, bibī	I drink
clāmor, clāmōris, m.	shout	cōnsilium capiō	I adopt a plan
cōnsilium, cōnsiliī, n.	plan	dēbeō, dēbēre, dēbuī, dēbitum	I ought, owe
custōs, custōdis, c.	guard	grātiās agō	I give thanks
hasta, hastae, f.	spear	interficiō, interficere, interfēcī, interfectum	I kill
hortus, hortī, m.	garden		
vōx, vōcis, f.	voice		
Adjectives		**Adverbs**	
clārus, -a, -um	famous	deinde	then
dexter, dextra, dextrum	right	iam	now, already
sinister, sinistra, sinistrum	left	iterum	again

So you really want to learn Latin...

Exercise 10. 8
Study the information on the opposite page about using the principal parts. Copying the format given for dēbeō, write out the principal parts and six tenses of the following:

1. rogō
2. discō
3. interficiō
4. dō
5. veniō
6. pellō

Exercise 10. 9
Revision: tenses. Translate the following:

1. surrēxit
2. pepulistī
3. cēlāre
4. discessī
5. frēgistis
6. cōnsilium cēpit
7. invēnērunt
8. lēgistī
9. vēnerant
10. cupient
11. cucurrerint
12. mīserat
13. fuit
14. didicit
15. dēscendet
16. sedent

Exercise 10. 10
Translate into English:

ōlim hostēs cum cōpiīs Rōmānīs pugnābant. diū mīlitēs pugnābant, nec tamen superāvērunt. tandem puer, nōmine Mūcius, rēgem interficere cōnstituit. gladium cēlāvit et in castra ambulāvit. deinde custōdem rēgis interfēcit.
  'quis es?' inquit rēx īrātus. 'cūr custōdem meum interfēcistī?'
  'mīles Rōmānus sum,' inquit Mūcius 'nec dolōrem timeō.'

dolor, dolōris m. = pain

Exercise 10. 11
From which Latin words do the following English ones derive? N.B. they are not all from Vocabulary 10. Explain the meaning of the English word and translate the Latin one.

1. Imbibe
2. Vocal
3. Decapitate
4. Capture
5. Debit
6. Dexterity
7. Duct
8. Ignite
9. Interrogate
10. Custody

Using Latin

sinister
sinister = left. In the ancient world things on the left were often considered unlucky or sinister.

The escape of Cloelia, 508 B.C.

Just before Lars Porsenna decided to give up fighting against the Romans, another piece of Roman behaviour helped to make up his mind for him once and for all. Mucius Scaevola sticking his hand in the flames was one thing. But when Roman maidens began swimming across fast flowing rivers…

During the war with Rome, Lars Porsenna had captured a large number of prisoners of war, some of whom were young girls. One day, one of these girls decided that she had had enough Etruscan food and wished to return to Rome. So she and a number of others broke out of the Etruscan camp, where they were being held, and crept down to the river. Then they all swam across the river and returned safely to Rome.

But there was a problem. The Romans had recently concluded a truce with Lars Porsenna and could not allow Roman prisoners to escape without breaking the truce. Cloelia and her friends had been very brave, but they had broken a truce and there was thus no alternative but to send them back. So back they went.

Once more, though, Lars Porsenna was hugely impressed by the Roman character. Bravery he had seen in abundance. But such honesty and integrity! Clearly he was out of his class when dealing with the Romans. So he sent Cloelia back to Rome, together with many more prisoners than had escaped. And very soon after this the war which he had been waging against Rome on behalf of Tarquinius Superbus was abandoned and he trotted off back to Clusium.

So you really want to learn Latin…

Exercise 10. 12

Read the story of Cloelia on the opposite page. Then answer the following questions:

1. Tell the story of Cloelia in your own words.
2. Which qualities would the Romans be trying to encourage in their children by telling them the story of Cloelia? Explain your answer.
3. Why do you think Lars Porsenna decided to end his war with Rome as a result of the Cloelia episode?
4. From what you have learnt about the Romans so far, write a list of adjectives to describe the model Roman?

Exercise 10. 13

So, you made it? You got to the end of Book I unscathed and are now pretty hot at Latin? Well, just to check that you have been paying attention, explain the following expressions:

1. sine quā nōn
2. post mortem
3. magnum opus
4. in locō parentis
5. tempus fugit
6. alibī
7. festīnā lentē
8. post scrīptum
9. et cētera
10. terra firma

And for a little light relief, there is an end of Book 1 quiz to have a go at on the YouTube channel.

Using Latin

fīnis
In Latin, fīnis = the end!

SUMMARY OF GRAMMAR

Verbs

Present infinitive: To love

| amāre | monēre | regere | audīre | capere |

Present: *I love, I am loving, I do love*

amō	moneō	regō	audiō	capiō
amās	monēs	regis	audīs	capis
amat	monet	regit	audit	capit
amāmus	monēmus	regimus	audīmus	capimus
amātis	monētis	regitis	audītis	capitis
amant	monent	regunt	audiunt	capiunt

Future: *I shall love, I will love*

amābō	monēbō	regam	audiam	capiam
amābis	monēbis	regēs	audiēs	capiēs
amābit	monēbit	reget	audiet	capiet
amābimus	monēbimus	regēmus	audiēmus	capiēmus
amābitis	monēbitis	regētis	audiētis	capiētis
amābunt	monēbunt	regent	audient	capient

Imperfect: *I was loving, I loved, I used to love*

amābam	monēbam	regēbam	audiēbam	capiēbam
amābās	monēbās	regēbās	audiēbās	capiēbās
amābat	monēbat	regēbat	audiēbat	capiēbat
amābāmus	monēbāmus	regēbāmus	audiēbāmus	capiēbāmus
amābātis	monēbātis	regēbātis	audiēbātis	capiēbātis
amābant	monēbant	regēbant	audiēbant	capiēbant

Perfect: *I have loved, I loved*

amāvī	monuī	rēxī	audīvī	cēpī
amāvistī	monuistī	rēxistī	audīvistī	cēpistī
amāvit	monuit	rēxit	audīvit	cēpit
amāvimus	monuimus	rēximus	audīvimus	cēpimus
amāvistis	monuistis	rēxistis	audīvistis	cēpistis
amāvērunt	monuērunt	rēxērunt	audīvērunt	cēpērunt

Future perfect: *I shall have loved, I will have loved*

amāverō	monuerō	rēxerō	audīverō	cēperō
amāveris	monueris	rēxeris	audīveris	cēperis
amāverit	monuerit	rēxerit	audīverit	cēperit
amāverimus	monuerimus	rēxerimus	audīverimus	cēperimus
amāveritis	monueritis	rēxeritis	audīveritis	cēperitis
amāverint	monuerint	rēxerint	audīverint	cēperint

Pluperfect: *I had loved*

amāveram	monueram	rēxeram	audīveram	cēperam
amāverās	monuerās	rēxerās	audīverās	cēperās
amāverat	monuerat	rēxerat	audīverat	cēperat
amāverāmus	monuerāmus	rēxerāmus	audīverāmus	cēperāmus
amāverātis	monuerātis	rēxerātis	audīverātis	cēperātis
amāverant	monuerant	rēxerant	audīverant	cēperant

Irregular verb: sum, esse, fuī = I am

Present	Future	Imperfect
sum	erō	eram
es	eris	erās
est	erit	erat
sumus	erimus	erāmus
estis	eritis	erātis
sunt	erunt	erant

Nouns

1st declension

Nominative	mēnsa	Table (subject)
Vocative	mēnsa	O table
Accusative	mēnsam	Table (object)
Genitive	mēnsae	Of a table
Dative	mēnsae	To, for a table
Ablative	mēnsā	By, with or from a table
Nominative	mēnsae	Tables (subject)
Vocative	mēnsae	O tables
Accusative	mēnsās	Tables (object)
Genitive	mēnsārum	Of the tables
Dative	mēnsīs	To, for the tables
Ablative	mēnsīs	By, with or from the tables

2nd declension

Nominative	annus	puer	magister	bellum
Vocative	anne	puer	magister	bellum
Accusative	annum	puerum	magistrum	bellum
Genitive	annī	puerī	magistrī	bellī
Dative	annō	puerō	magistrō	bellō
Ablative	annō	puerō	magistrō	bellō
Nominative	annī	puerī	magistrī	bella
Vocative	annī	puerī	magistrī	bella
Accusative	annōs	puerōs	magistrōs	bella
Genitive	annōrum	puerōrum	magistrōrum	bellōrum
Dative	annīs	puerīs	magistrīs	bellīs
Ablative	annīs	puerīs	magistrīs	bellīs

2nd declension Irregular

Nominative	fīlius	deus	vir
Vocative	fīlī	deus	vir
Accusative	fīlium	deum	virum
Genitive	fīlī (fīliī)	deī	virī
Dative	fīliō	deō	virō
Ablative	fīliō	deō	virō
Nominative	fīliī	dī (deī)	virī
Vocative	fīliī	dī (deī)	virī
Accusative	fīliōs	deōs	virōs
Genitive	fīliōrum	deōrum (deum)	virōrum (virum)
Dative	fīliīs	dīs (deīs)	virīs
Ablative	fīliīs	dīs (deīs)	virīs

Nouns (cont.)
3rd declension

Nominative	rēx	opus	cīvis	cubīle
Vocative	rēx	opus	cīvis	cubīle
Accusative	rēgem	opus	cīvem	cubīle
Genitive	rēgis	operis	cīvis	cubīlis
Dative	rēgī	operī	cīvī	cubīlī
Ablative	rēge	opere	cīve	cubīlī
Nominative	rēgēs	opera	cīvēs	cubīlia
Vocative	rēgēs	opera	cīvēs	cubīlia
Accusative	rēgēs	opera	cīvēs	cubīlia
Genitive	rēgum	operum	cīvium	cubīlium
Dative	rēgibus	operibus	cīvibus	cubīlibus
Ablative	rēgibus	operibus	cīvibus	cubīlibus

Cardinal Numerals

1	I	ūnus		30	XXX	trīgintā
2	II	duŏ		40	XL	quadrāgintā
3	III	trēs		50	L	quīnquāgintā
4	IV/IIII	quattuor		60	LX	sexāgintā
5	V	quīnque		70	LXX	septuāgintā
6	VI	sex		80	LXXX	octōgintā
7	VII	septem		90	XC	nōnāgintā
8	VIII	octŏ		100	C	centum
9	IX	novem		500	D	quīngentī
10	X	decem		1000	M	mīlle
11	XI	ūndecim				
12	XII	duodecim				
13	XIII	tredecim				
14	XIV	quattuordecim				
15	XV	quīndecim				
16	XVI	sēdecim				
17	XVII	septendecim				
18	XVIII	duodēvīgintī				
19	XIX	ūndēvīgintī				
20	XX	vīgintī				

Ordinals

1st	prīmus		6th	sextus
2nd	secundus		7th	septimus
3rd	tertius		8th	octāvus
4th	quārtus		9th	nōnus
5th	quīntus		10th	decimus

Adjectives
1st / 2nd declension in -us

	M	F	N
Nominative	bonus	bona	bonum
Vocative	bone	bona	bonum
Accusative	bonum	bonam	bonum
Genitive	bonī	bonae	bonī
Dative	bonō	bonae	bonō
Ablative	bonō	bonā	bonō
Nominative	bonī	bonae	bona
Vocative	bonī	bonae	bona
Accusative	bonōs	bonās	bona
Genitive	bonōrum	bonārum	bonōrum
Dative	bonīs	bonīs	bonīs
Ablative	bonīs	bonīs	bonīs

1st / 2nd declension in -er

	M	F	N	M	F	N
Nom.	tener	tenera	tenerum	pulcher	pulchra	pulchrum
Voc.	tener	tenera	tenerum	pulcher	pulchra	pulchrum
Acc.	tenerum	teneram	tenerum	pulchrum	pulchram	pulchrum
Gen.	tenerī	tenerae	tenerī	pulchrī	pulchrae	pulchrī
Dat.	tenerō	tenerae	tenerō	pulchrō	pulchrae	pulchrō
Abl.	tenerō	tenerā	tenerō	pulchrō	pulchrā	pulchrō
Nom.	tenerī	tenerae	tenera	pulchrī	pulchrae	pulchra
Voc.	tenerī	tenerae	tenera	pulchrī	pulchrae	pulchra
Acc.	tenerōs	tenerās	tenera	pulchrōs	pulchrās	pulchra
Gen.	tenerōrum	tenerārum	tenerōrum	pulchrōrum	pulchrārum	pulchrōrum
Dat.	tenerīs	tenerīs	tenerīs	pulchrīs	pulchrīs	pulchrīs
Abl.	tenerīs	tenerīs	tenerīs	pulchrīs	pulchrīs	pulchrīs

APPENDIX

More on vowel quantity

It is a brave man who inserts a macron over a vowel in a book which is to be read by people outside his immediate family. Or chooses not to do so, for that matter. Just think of the hoots of derision that will be heard, ringing through the countryside, as the errors are spotted and chortled over.

Well, just to make clear what I have done, or attempted to do, here are a few notes. I am for ever in debt to Theo Zinn, with whom I defy anyone to argue on matters of quantity. Theo taught me everything I know and many a happy hour has been spent in his company, looking up obscure references in search of the answers to some of the more niggling problems of Latin vowel quantity, but no doubt you will all have your own views on my decisions.

1. Vowels are marked as long where they are known to be long.

2. Vowels are sometimes marked as short where the tendency to get them wrong is so distressing as to require correction (thus egŏ).

3. Vowels are marked as anceps (= ambiguous) where the vowel could be pronounced either long or short, as in: octŏ̄, homŏ̄, quandŏ̄, ibĭ̄ and ubĭ̄.

4. Consonant i: Both Allen (Vox Latina, p. 38-9) and Kennedy (Revised Latin Primer, p. 42, note 3) agree that consonant i between two vowels was pronounced as a doubled consonant and thus that while the preceding vowel was short, the syllable always *scans* long. Books which thus *mark* words such as maior, peior, Troia, etc. as having a long first syllable are presumably doing so for the benefit of pupils writing or scanning verse. But if macrons are there principally to aid pronunciation, as in a book of this sort, they are clearly most misleading if inserted over what are in fact agreed to be short vowels.

5. Vowels before ns and nf are always long, even (as Allen tells us, p. 65, note 2) at word junction. Thus the need to mark the i of īn sitū, for example, as long.

6. Latin words which have become, by adoption, English ones have caused me some difficulty in the *Using Latin* boxes. I have had to decide whether to write a word such as *alias* as a Latin word, with macrons where appropriate, or as an English one (and thus with no macrons). My policy here, such as it is, has been always to give the Latin word at the top, correctly marked, but to show the word unmarked in the explanation where it has become so much a part of the English language as to have lost its Latin quality altogether. Such words as *via, alibi* and *extra* would fit into this category, whereas phrases such as status quō would not.

Latin – English Vocabulary

(Including all words used in this book, together with some additional, commonly-used words)

ā, ab + abl. = by, from
absum, abesse, āfuī = I am absent
ad + acc. = to, towards
adsum, adesse, adfuī = I am present
aedificō, -āre, -āvī, -ātum = I build
ager, agrī, m. = field
agō, agere, ēgī, āctum = I do
agricola, -ae, m. = farmer
altus, -a, -um = deep, high
ambulō, -āre, -āvī, -ātum = I walk
amīcus, -ī, m. = friend
amō, amāre, amāvī, amātum = I love, like
animal, animālis, n. = animal
annus, -ī, m. = year
ante + acc. = before
aperiō, -īre, aperuī, apertum = I open
appellō, -āre, -āvī, -ātum = I call
appropinquō, -āre, -āvī, -ātum = I approach
aqua, -ae, f. = water
arbor, -ŏris, f. = tree
arma, -ōrum, n. pl. = weapons
ars, artis, f. = skill, art
ascendō, -ere, ascendī, ascēnsum = I climb
ātrium, ātriī, n. = hall (of a house)
audiō, -īre, -īvī, -ītum = I hear, listen to
aurum, -ī, n. = gold
autem = however, moreover
auxilium, -iī, n. = help
barbarus, -a, -um = barbarian (adjective)
barbarus, -ī, m. = barbarian (noun)
bellum, -ī, n. = war
bene = well
bibō, -ere, bibī = I drink
bonus, -a, -um = good
cadō, -ere, cecidī, cāsum = I fall
caelum, -ī, n. = sky
cantō, -āre, -āvī, -ātum = I sing
capiō, -ere, cēpī, captum = I take, capture

caput, -itis, n. = head
carmen, carminis, n. = poem, song
castra, -ōrum, n. pl. = camp
cecidī: see **cadō**
cēlō, -āre, -āvī, -ātum = I hide
cēna, -ae, f. = dinner
centum = one hundred
cēpī: see **capiō**
cibus, -ī, m. = food
circum + acc. = around
cīvis, cīvis, c. = citizen
clāmō, -āre, -āvī, -ātum = I shout
clāmor, -ōris, m. = shout
clārus, -a, -um = famous
claudō, claudere, clausī, clausum = I close
coēgī: see **cōgō**
cōgō, cōgere, coēgī, coāctum = I compel, force
cōnsilium capiō = I adopt a plan
cōnsilium, -iī, n. = plan
cōnstituō, -ere, -stituī, -stitūtum = I decide
cōnsul, cōnsulis, m. = consul
contrā + acc. = against
cōpiae, -ārum, f. pl. = forces
corpus, -ŏris, n. = body
crās = tomorrow
cubīle, cubīlis, n. = bed
cucurrī: see **currō**
cum + abl. = with, together with
cupiō, -ere, -īvī, -ītum = I want, desire
cūr? = why?
cūrō, -āre, -āvī, -ātum = I care for
currō, -ere, cucurrī, cursum = I run
custōs, custōdis, c. = guard
dē + abl. = down from, concerning
dea, -ae, f. = goddess (dat. and abl. pl. = **deābus**)
dēbeō, -ēre, -uī, -itum = I ought, owe
decem = ten
dedī: see **dō**

deinde = then
dēlectō, -āre, -āvī, -ātum = I delight, please
dēleō, dēlēre, dēlēvī, dēlētum = I destroy
dēscendō, -ere, -scendī, -scēnsum = I go down
deus, deī, m. (irreg.) = god
dexter, -tra, -trum = right
dīcō, dīcere, dīxī, dictum = I say
discēdō, -ere, discessī, discessum = I depart
discō, discere, didicī = I learn
diū = for a long time
dīxī: see **dīcō**
dō, dăre, dedī, dătum = I give
doceō, -ēre, docuī, doctum = I teach
doleō, -ēre, doluī, dolitum = I feel pain, am sad
dolor, dolōris, m. = pain
dominus, -ī, m. = master, lord
dōnum, -ī, n. = gift
dormiō, -īre, -īvī, -ītum = I sleep
dūcō, -ere, dūxī, ductum = I lead
dum = while
duŏ = two
duodecim = twelve
duodēvīgintī = eighteen
dux, ducis, c. = leader
ē, ex + abl. = out of
ecce = look!
ēgī: see **agō**
egŏ = I
enim = for
equus, equī, m. = horse
errō, -āre, -āvī, -ātum = I wander, err, make a mistake
esse: see **sum**
et = and
et...et = both...and
ex + abl. = out of
exspectō, -āre, -āvī, -ātum = I wait for
fābula, -ae, f. = story
faciō, -ere, fēcī, factum = I do, make
fāma, -ae, f. = fame, glory
fēcī: see **faciō**
fēmina, -ae, f. = woman

fessus, -a, -um = tired
festīnō, -āre, -āvī, -ātum = I hurry
fīlia, -ae, f. = daughter (dat. and abl. pl. = **fīliābus**)
fīlius, fīliī (or fīlī), m. (irreg.) = son
fleō, flēre, flēvī, flētum = I weep
flōs, flōris, m. = flower
flūmen, flūminis, n. = river
fōns, fontis, m. = fountain
forte = by chance
forum, -ī, n. = forum
frangō, -ere, frēgī, frāctum = I break
frāter, frātris, m. = brother
frēgī: see **frangō**
frūstrā = in vain
fuga, -ae, f. = flight, escape
fugiō, -ere, fūgī = I flee
fuī: see **sum**
gēns, gentis, f. = people, race,
gerō, -ere, gessī, gestum = I manage, wage (a war), wear
gessī: see **gerō**
gladius, gladiī, m. = sword
Graecia, -ae, f. = Greece
grātiās agō = I give thanks
habeō, -ēre -uī, -itum = I have
habitō, -āre, -āvī, -ātum = I live, inhabit
hasta, -ae, f. = spear
herba, -ae, f. = grass
hīc = here
homŏ, hominis, c. = man, person
hortus, -ī, m. = garden
hostis, hostis, c. = enemy (usually used in plural)
iaciō, -ere, iēcī, iactum = I throw
iam = now, already
ibĭ = there
iēcī: see **iaciō**
igitur = therefore
ignis, ignis, m = fire
imperium, -iī, n. = command, empire
in + abl. = in, on
in + acc. = into, on to
incendō, -ere, incendī, incēnsum = I burn
incola, -ae, c. = inhabitant
inde = then

īnsula, -ae, f. = island
inter + acc. = between, among
interficiō, -ere, interfēcī, interfectum = I kill
intrō, -āre, -āvī, -ātum = I enter
inveniō, -īre, invēnī, inventum = I find
īra, -ae, f. = anger
īrātus, -a, -um = angry
ita = thus
Ītalia, -ae, f. = Italy
itaque = therefore
iter, itineris, n. = journey
iterum = again
iubeō, -ēre, iussī, iussum = I order
iūdex, iūdicis, c. = judge
iuvenis, iuvenis, m. = young man
labōrō, -āre, -āvī, -ātum = I work
laetus, -a, -um = happy
laudō, -āre, -āvī, -ātum = I praise
legō, -ere, lēgī, lēctum = I read, choose
liber, librī, m. = book
locus, -ī, m. = place
longus, -a, -um = long
lūdō, -ere, lūsī, lūsum = I play
lūdus, -ī, m. = school
lūsī: see **lūdō**
lūx, lūcis, f. = light
magister, magistrī, m. = master (schoolmaster)
magnopere = greatly
magnus, -a, -um = big, great
malus, -a, -um = bad
maneō, -ēre, mānsī, mānsum = I remain
mare, maris, n. = sea
māter, mātris, f. = mother
mātrimōnium, -iī, n. = marriage
medius, -a, -um = middle
mēnsa, mēnsae, f. = table
meus, -a, -um = my
mīles, mīlitis, c. = soldier
mīlle = one thousand
miser, -era, -erum = wretched
mīsī: see **mittō**
mittō, -ere, mīsī, missum = I send
moneō, -ēre, -uī, -itum = I warn, advise
mōns, montis, m. = mountain
mors, mortis, f. = death
moveō, -ēre, mōvī, mōtum = I move, set in motion
mox = soon
multus, -a, -um = much, many
mūrus, -ī, m. = wall
nam = for
nārrō, -āre, -āvī, -ātum = I tell
nauta, -ae, m. = sailor
nāvigō, -āre, -āvī, -ātum = I sail
nāvis, nāvis, f. = ship
-ne? : introduces a question
nec = and not, nor
nec tamen = but...not
nec...nec = neither...nor
necō, necāre, necāvī, necātum = I kill
neque = and not, nor
neque tamen = but...not
neque...neque = neither...nor
niger, nigra, nigrum = black
nōmen, nōminis, n. = name
nōn = not
nōnne?: introduces a question (expecting the answer 'yes')
nōs = we
noster, nostra, nostrum = our
nōtus, -a, -um = well-known
novem = nine
novus, -a, -um = new
nox, noctis, f. = night
num?: introduces a question (expecting the answer 'no')
numquam = never
nūntius, nūntiī, m. = messenger, message
occīdo, -ere, occīdī, occīsum = I kill
octō = eight
oculus, -ī, m. = eye
ōlim = once upon a time
oppidum, -ī, n. = town
oppugnō, -āre, -āvī, -ātum = I attack (a city or camp)
opus, operis, n. = work
ōra, -ae, f. = shore
ōrō, -āre, -āvī, -ātum = I beg, pray
ostendō, -ere, ostendī, ostēnsum / ostentum = I show
parō, -āre, -āvī, -ātum = I prepare

parvus, -a, -um = small
pater, patris, m. = father
patria, -ae, f. = country, fatherland
pecūnia, -ae, f. = money
pellō, -ere, pepulī, pulsum = I drive
per + acc. = through, along
perīculum, -ī, n. = danger
poēta, -ae, m. = poet
pōnō, -ere, posuī, positum = I place
pōns, pontis, m. = bridge
populus, -ī, m. = a people
porta, -ae, f. = gate
portō, -āre, -āvī, -ātum = I carry
post + acc. = after
posteā = afterwards
pretium, -iī, n. = price
proelium, -iī, n. = battle
prope + acc. = near
puella, -ae, f. = girl
puer, puerī, m. = boy
pugna, -ae, f. = battle, fight
pugnō, -āre, -āvī, -ātum = I fight
pulcher, -chra, -chrum = beautiful
quaerō, -ere, quaesīvī, quaesītum = I ask, seek
quandŏ̄ = when?
quattuor = four
quattuordecim = fourteen
quid? = what?
quīndecim = fifteen
quīnque = five
quis? = who?
quōmodŏ? = how?
quot? = how many?
reddō, reddere, reddidī, redditum = I return, give back
redūcō, -ere, redūxī, reductum = I lead back
regō, -ere, rēxī, rēctum = I rule
respondeō, -ēre, respondī, respōnsum = I reply, answer
reveniō, -īre, revēnī, reventum = I return, come back
rēx, rēgis, m. = king
rēxī: see **regō**
rīdeō, -ēre, rīsī, rīsum = I laugh, smile
rīpa, -ae, f. = riverbank
rogō, -āre, -āvī, -ātum = I ask

Rōma, -ae, f. = Rome
Rōmānus, -a, -um = Roman (adjective)
Rōmānus, -ī, m. = Roman (noun)
ruō, ruere, ruī, rutum = I rush
sacer, sacra, sacrum = sacred
saepe = often
saevus, -a, -um = savage
sagitta, -ae, f. = arrow
salūtō, -āre, -āvī, -ātum = I greet
salvē, salvēte = hello, greetings
sapientia, -ae, f. = wisdom
scrībō, -ere, scrīpsī, scrīptum = I write
scūtum, -ī, n. = shield
sed = but
sēdecim = sixteen
sedeō, sedēre, sēdī, sessum = I sit
semper = always
senex, senis, m. = old man
septem = seven
septendecim = seventeen
servō, -āre, -āvī, -ātum = I save
servus, -ī, m. = slave
sex = six
sī = if
sīc = thus
silva, -ae, f. = wood, forest
sine + abl. = without
sinister, -tra, -trum = left
socius, -iī, m. = ally
sōl, sōlis, m. = sun
spectō, -āre, -āvī, -ātum = I watch
statim = immediately
stetī: see **stō**
stō, stāre, stetī, stătum = I stand
sub + abl. = under
subitō = suddenly
sum, esse, fuī (irreg.) = I am
super + acc. = over
superbus, -a, -um = proud
superō, -āre, -āvī, -ātum = I overcome
surgō, -ere, surrēxī, surrēctum = I rise, get up
tamen = however
tandem = at last, at length
tēlum, -ī, n. = spear, missile
tempestās, tempestātis, f. = storm, weather
tempus, -ŏris, n. = time

teneō, -ēre, tenuī, tentum = I hold
tener, -era, -erum = tender
terra, -ae, f. = land, earth
terreō, -ēre, -uī, -itum = I terrify
theātrum, -ī, n. = theatre
timeō, -ēre, -uī = I fear
trādō, -ere, trādidī, trāditum = I hand over
trahō, -ere, trāxī, tractum = I drag
trāns + acc. = across
tredecim = thirteen
trēs = three
Troia, -ae, f. = Troy
tū = you (singular)
tum = then
tūtus, -a, -um = safe
tuus, -a, -um = your
ubĭ = when; where
ubĭ? = where?
unda, -ae, f. = wave
ūndecim = eleven
ūndēvīgintī = nineteen

ūnus, -a, -um = one
urbs, urbis, f. = city
uxor, -ōris, f. = wife
validus, -a, -um = strong
veniō, -īre, vēnī, ventum = I come
ventus, -ī, m. = wind
verberō, -āre, -āvi, -ātum = I beat, hit
verbum, -ī, n. = word
vester, vestra, vestrum = your
via, -ae, f. = road, street, way
victōria, -ae, f. = victory
videō, -ēre, vīdī, vīsum = I see
vīgintī = twenty
vir, virī, m. (irreg.) = man
virtūs, virtūtis, f. = courage
vītō, -āre, -āvī, -ātum = I avoid
vocō, -āre, -āvī, -ātum = I call
vōs = you (plural)
vōx, vōcis, f. = voice
vulnerō, -āre, -āvī, -ātum = I wound
vulnus, vulneris, n. = wound

English – Latin Vocabulary

(Including all words used in this book, together with some additional, commonly-used words)

About (concerning) = **dē** + abl.
Absent, I am = **absum, abesse, āfuī**
Across = **trāns** + acc.
Advise, I = **moneō, -ēre, -uī, -itum**
After = **post** + acc.
Afterwards = **posteā**
Again = **iterum**
Against = **contrā** + acc.
Ally = **socius, -iī,** m.
Already = **iam**
Always = **semper**
Am, I = **sum, esse, fuī** (irreg.)
Among = **inter** + acc.
And = **et**
And...not = **nec; neque**
Anger = **īra, -ae,** f.
Angry = **īrātus, -a, -um**
Animal = **animal, animālis,** n.
Answer, I = **respondeō, -ēre, respondī, respōnsum**
Approach, I = **appropinquō, -āre, -āvī, -ātum**
Arms (weapons) = **arma, -ōrum,** n. pl.
Around = **circum** + acc.
Arrow = **sagitta, -ae,** f.
Art = **ars, artis,** f.
Ask, I = **rogō, -āre, -āvī, -ātum**
At last = **tandem**
Attack (a city or camp), I = **oppugnō, -āre, -āvī, -ātum**
Avoid, I = **vītō, -āre, -āvī, -ātum**
Bad = **malus, -a, -um**
Bank = **rīpa, -ae,** f.
Barbarian (noun) = **barbarus, -ī,** m.
 (adjective) = **barbarus, -a, -um**
Battle = **pugna, -ae,** f.; **proelium, -iī,** n.
Beat, I = **verberō, -āre, -āvī, -ātum**
Beautiful = **pulcher, -chra, -chrum**
Bed = **cubīle, cubīlis,** n.
Before = **ante** + acc.
Between = **inter** + acc.
Big = **magnus, -a, -um**
Black = **niger, nigra, nigrum**

Body = **corpus, -ŏris,** n.
Book = **liber, librī,** m.
Both...and = **et...et**
Boy = **puer, puerī,** m.
Break, I = **frangō, -ere, frēgī, frāctum**
Bridge = **pōns, pontis,** m.
Brother = **frāter, frātris,** m.
Build, I = **aedificō, -āre, -āvī, -ātum**
Burn, I = **incendō, -ere, incendī, incēnsum**
But = **sed**
But...not = **nec tamen; neque tamen**
By = **ā, ab** + abl.
By chance = **forte**
Call, I = **vocō, -āre, -āvī, -ātum**
Call (by name), I = **appellō, -āre, -āvī, -ātum**
Camp = **castra, -ōrum,** n. pl.
Capture, I = **capiō, -ere, cēpī, captum**
Care for, I = **cūrō, -āre, -āvī, -ātum**
Carry, I = **portō, -āre, -āvī, -ātum**
Choose, I = **legō, -ere, lēgī, lēctum**
Citizen = **cīvis, cīvis,** c.
City = **urbs, urbis,** f.
Climb, I = **ascendō, -ere, ascendī, ascēnsum**
Close, I = **claudō, claudere, clausī, clausum**
Come, I = **veniō, -īre, vēnī, ventum**
Command (noun) = **imperium, -iī,** n.
Compel, I = **cōgō, cōgere, coēgī, coāctum**
Concerning = **dē** + abl.
Consul = **cōnsul, cōnsulis,** m.
Country = **patria, -ae,** f.
Courage = **virtūs, virtūtis,** f.
Danger = **perīculum, -ī,** n.
Daughter = **fīlia, -ae,** f. (dat. and abl. pl. = **fīliābus**)
Death = **mors, mortis,** f.
Decide, I = **cōnstituō, -ere, -stituī, -stitūtum**
Deep = **altus, -a, -um**

Delight, I = **dēlectō, -āre, -āvī, -ātum**
Depart, I = **discēdō, -ere, discessī, discessum**
Desire, I = **cupiō, -ere, -īvī, -ītum**
Destroy, I = **dēleō, dēlēre, dēlēvī, dēlētum**
Dinner = **cēna, -ae, f.**
Do, I = **faciō, -ere, fēci, factum; agō, agere, ēgī, āctum**
Down from = **dē** + abl.
Drag, I = **trahō, -ere, trāxī, tractum**
Drink, I = **bibō, -ere, bibī**
Drive, I = **pellō, -ere, pepulī, pulsum**
Eight = **octŏ**
Eighteen = **duodēvīgintī**
Eleven = **ūndecim**
Empire = **imperium, -iī, n.**
Enemy = **hostis, hostis,** c. (usually used in plural)
Enter, I = **intrō, -āre, -āvī, -ātum**
Eye = **oculus, -ī, m.**
Fall, I = **cadō, -ere, cecidī, cāsum**
Fame = **fāma, -ae, f.**
Famous = **clārus, -a, -um**
Farmer = **agricola, -ae, m.**
Father = **pater, patris, m.**
Fatherland = **patria, -ae, f.**
Fear, I = **timeō, -ēre, -uī**
Field = **ager, agrī, m.**
Fifteen = **quīndecim**
Fight (noun) = **pugna, -ae, f.**
Fight, I = **pugnō, -āre, -āvī, -ātum**
Find, I = **inveniō, -īre, invēnī, inventum**
Five = **quīnque**
Flee, I = **fugiō, -ere, fūgī**
Flight = **fuga, -ae, f.**
Flower = **flōs, flōris, m.**
Food = **cibus, -ī, m.**
For = **nam; enim** (2nd word in clause)
For a long time = **diū**
Force, I = **cōgō, cōgere, coēgī, coāctum**
Forces = **cōpiae, -ārum, f. pl.**
Forum = **forum, -ī, n.**
Fountain = **fōns, fontis, m.**
Four = **quattuor**
Fourteen = **quattuordecim**

Friend = **amīcus, -ī, m.**
From = **ā, ab** + abl.
Garden = **hortus, -ī, m.**
Gate = **porta, -ae, f.**
Gift = **dōnum, -ī, n.**
Girl = **puella, -ae, f.**
Give back, I = **reddō, reddere, reddidī, redditum**
Give, I = **dō, dăre, dedī, dătum**
Glory = **fāma, -ae, f.**
Go down, I = **dēscendō, -ere, -scendī, -scēnsum**
Go in, I = **intrō, -āre, -āvī, -ātum**
God = **deus, deī,** m. (irreg.)
Goddess = **dea, -ae,** f. (dat. and abl. pl. = **deābus**)
Gold = **aurum, -ī, n.**
Good = **bonus, -a, -um**
Grass = **herba, -ae, f.**
Great = **magnus, -a, -um**
Greatly = **magnopere**
Greece = **Graecia, -ae, f.**
Greet, I = **salūtō, -āre, -āvī, -ātum**
Ground = **terra, -ae, f.**
Guard (noun) = **custōs, custōdis, c.**
Hall (of a house) = **ātrium, ātriī, n.**
Hand over, I = **trādō, -ere, trādidī, trāditum**
Happy = **laetus, -a, -um**
Have, I = **habeō, -ēre, -uī, -itum**
Head = **caput, -itis, n.**
Hear, I = **audiō, -īre, -īvī, -ītum**
Hello = **salvē, salvēte**
Help = **auxilium, -iī, n.**
Here = **hīc**
Hide, I = **cēlō, -āre, -āvī, -ātum**
High = **altus, -a, -um**
Hold, I = **teneō, -ēre, tenuī, tentum**
Horse = **equus, equī, m.**
How many? = **quot?**
How? = **quōmodŏ?**
However = **autem; tamen** (both 2nd word in clause)
Hundred, one = **centum**
Hurry, I = **festīnō, -āre, -āvī, -ātum**
I = **egō**
If = **sī**

Immediately = **statim**
In = **in** + abl.
In vain = **frūstrā**
Inhabitant = **incola, -ae,** c.
Into = **in** + acc.
Island = **īnsula, -ae,** f.
Italy = **Ītalia, -ae,** f.
Journey = **iter, itineris,** n.
Judge = **iūdex, iūdicis,** c.
Kill, I = **necō, necāre, necāvī, necātum; interficiō, -ere, interfēcī, interfectum; occīdō, -ere, occīdī, occīsum**
King = **rēx, rēgis,** m.
Land = **terra, -ae,** f.
Laugh, I = **rīdeō, -ēre, rīsī, rīsum**
Lead, I = **dūcō, -ere, dūxī, ductum**
Lead back, I = **redūcō, -ere, redūxī, reductum**
Leader = **dux, ducis,** c.
Left = **sinister, -tra, -trum**
Light = **lūx, lūcis,** f.
Like, I = **amō, amāre, amāvī, amātum**
Listen to, I = **audiō, -īre, -īvī, -ītum**
Live (inhabit), I = **habitō, -āre, -āvī, -ātum**
Long = **longus, -a, -um**
Look at, I = **spectō, -āre, -āvī, -ātum**
Look! = **ecce**
Lord = **dominus, -ī,** m.
Love, I = **amō, amāre, amāvī, amātum**
Make, I = **faciō, -ere, fēcī, factum**
Man (as opposed to woman) = **vir, virī,** m. (irreg.); (person) = **homŏ, hominis,** c.
Manage, I = **gerō, -ere, gessī, gestum**
Many: see Much
Marriage = **mātrimōnium, -iī,** n.
Master (i.e. schoolmaster) = **magister, magistrī,** m.; (i.e. lord) = **dominus, -ī,** m.
Message = **nūntius, nūntiī,** m.
Messenger = **nūntius, nūntiī,** m.
Middle = **medius, -a, -um**
Missile = **tēlum, -ī,** n.
Money = **pecūnia, -ae,** f.
Moreover = **autem** (second word in clause)
Mother = **māter, mātris,** f.
Mountain = **mōns, montis,** m.
Move (set in motion), I = **moveō, -ēre, mōvī, mōtum**
Much = **multus, -a, -um**
My = **meus, -a, -um**
Name = **nōmen, nōminis,** n.
Near = **prope** + acc.
Neither...nor = **nec...nec; neque...neque**
Never = **numquam**
New = **novus, -a, -um**
Night = **nox, noctis,** f.
Nine = **novem**
Nineteen = **ūndēvīgintī**
Nor = **nec; neque**
Not = **nōn**
Now = **iam**
Often = **saepe**
Old man = **senex, senis,** m.
On = **in** + abl.
Once, once upon a time = **ōlim**
One = **ūnus, -a, -um**
On to = **in** + acc.
Open, I = **aperiō, -īre, aperuī, apertum**
Order, I = **iubeō, -ēre, iussī, iussum**
Ought, I = **dēbeō, -ēre, -uī, -itum**
Our = **noster, nostra, nostrum**
Out of = **ē / ex** + abl.
Over = **super** + acc.
Overcome, I = **superō, -āre, -āvī, -ātum**
Owe, I = **dēbeō, -ēre, -uī, -itum**
Pain = **dolor, dolōris,** m.
Pain, I feel = **doleō, -ēre, doluī, dolitum**
People (population) = **populus, -ī,** m.; (race, tribe) = **gēns, gentis,** f.
Person = **homŏ, hominis,** c.
Place (noun) = **locus, -ī,** m.
Place, I = **pōnō, -ere, posuī, positum**
Plan = **cōnsilium, -iī,** n.
Plan, I adopt a = **cōnsilium capiō**
Play, I = **lūdō, -ere, lūsī, lūsum**
Poem = **carmen, carminis,** n.
Poet = **poēta, -ae,** m.
Praise, I = **laudō, -āre, -āvī, -ātum**
Pray, I = **ōrō, -āre, -āvī, -ātum**
Prepare, I = **parō, -āre, -āvī, -ātum**
Present, I am = **adsum, adesse, adfuī**

Price = **pretium, -iī, n.**
Proud = **superbus, -a, -um**
Read, I = **legō, -ere, lēgī, lēctum**
Remain, I = **maneō, -ēre, mānsī, mānsum**
Reply, I = **respondeō, -ēre, respondī, respōnsum**
Return (come back), I = **reveniō, -īre, revēnī, reventum**; (give back), I = **reddō, reddere, reddidī, redditum**
Right (as opposed to left) = **dexter, -tra, -trum**
Rise, I = **surgō, -ere, surrēxī, surrēctum**
River = **flūmen, flūminis, n.**
Riverbank = **rīpa, -ae, f.**
Road = **via, -ae, f.**
Roman (adjective) = **Rōmānus, -a, -um** (noun) = **Rōmānus, -ī, m.**
Rome = **Rōma, -ae, f.**
Rule, I = **regō, -ere, rēxī, rēctum**
Run, I = **currō, -ere, cucurrī, cursum**
Rush, I = **ruō, ruere, ruī, rutum**
Sacred = **sacer, sacra, sacrum**
Sad, I am = **doleō, -ēre, doluī, dolitum**
Safe = **tūtus, -a, -um**
Sail, I = **nāvigō, -āre, -āvī, -ātum**
Sailor = **nauta, -ae, m.**
Savage = **saevus, -a, -um**
Save, I = **servō, -āre, -āvī, -ātum**
Say, I = **dīcō, dīcere, dīxī, dictum**
School = **lūdus, -ī, m.**
Schoolmaster = **magister, magistrī, m.**
Sea = **mare, maris, n.**
See, I = **videō, -ēre, vīdī, vīsum**
Seek, I = **quaerō, -ere, quaesīvī, quaesītum**
Send, I = **mittō, -ere, mīsī, missum**
Seven = **septem**
Seventeen = **septendecim**
Shield = **scūtum, -ī, n.**
Ship = **nāvis, nāvis, f.**
Shore = **ōra, -ae, f.**
Shout (noun) = **clāmor, -ōris, m.**
Shout, I = **clāmō, -āre, -āvī, -ātum**
Show, I = **ostendō, -ere, ostendī, ostēnsum / ostentum**
Sing, I = **cantō, -āre, -āvī, -ātum**
Sit, I = **sedeō, sedēre, sēdī, sessum**
Six = **sex**
Sixteen = **sēdecim**
Skill = **ars, artis, f.**
Sky = **caelum, -ī, n.**
Slave = **servus, -ī, m.**
Sleep, I = **dormiō, -īre, -īvī, -ītum**
Small = **parvus, -a, -um**
Smile, I = **rīdeō, -ēre, rīsī, rīsum**
Soldier = **mīles, mīlitis, c.**
Son = **fīlius, fīliī (or fīlī), m. (irreg.)**
Song = **carmen, carminis, n.**
Soon = **mox**
Spear = **hasta, -ae, f.; tēlum, -ī, n.**
Stand, I = **stō, stāre, stetī, stātum**
Story = **fābula, -ae, f.**
Street = **via, -ae, f.**
Strong = **validus, -a, -um**
Suddenly = **subitō**
Sun = **sōl, sōlis, m.**
Sword = **gladius, gladiī, m.**
Table = **mēnsa, mēnsae, f.**
Take (seize), I = **capiō, -ere, cēpī, captum**
Teach, I = **doceō, -ēre, docuī, doctum**
Tell (e.g. a story), I = **nārrō, -āre, -āvī, -ātum**
Ten = **decem**
Tender = **tener, -era, -erum**
Terrify, I = **terreō, -ēre, -uī, -itum**
Thanks, I give = **grātiās agō**
Theatre = **theātrum, -ī, n.**
Then = **deinde; inde; tum**
There = **ibī**
Therefore = **itaque; igitur** (2nd word in clause)
Thirteen = **tredecim**
Thousand = **mīlle**
Three = **trēs**
Through = **per** + acc.
Throw, I = **iaciō, -ere, iēcī, iactum**
Thus = **ita; sīc**
Time = **tempus, -ŏris, n.**
Tired = **fessus, -a, -um**
To, towards = **ad** + acc.
Together with = **cum** + abl.
Tomorrow = **crās**

Towards = **ad** + acc.
Town = **oppidum, -ī, n.**
Tree = **arbor, -ŏris, f.**
Troy = **Troia, -ae, f.**
Twelve = **duodecim**
Twenty = **vīgintī**
Two = **duŏ**
Under = **sub** + abl.
Victory = **victōria, -ae, f.**
Voice = **vōx, vōcis, f.**
Wage, I = **gerō, -ere, gessī, gestum**
Wait for, I = **exspectō, -āre, -āvī, -ātum**
Walk, I = **ambulō, -āre, -āvī, -ātum**
Wall = **mūrus, -ī, m.**
Wander, I = **errō, -āre, -āvī, -ātum**
Want, I = **cupiō, -ere, -īvī, -ītum**
War = **bellum, -ī, n.**
Warn, I = **moneō, -ēre, -uī, -itum**
Watch, I = **spectō, -āre, -āvī, -ātum**
Water = **aqua, -ae, f.**
Wave = **unda, -ae, f.**
Way = **via, -ae, f.**
We = **nōs**
Weapons = **arma, -ōrum, n. pl.**
Wear, I = **gerō, -ere, gessī, gestum**
Weep, I = **fleō, flēre, flēvī, flētum**
Well = **bene**
Well-known = **nōtus, -a, -um**
What? = **quid?**
When (conjunction) = **ubĭ**
When? (adverb) = **quandŏ?**
Where (conjunction) = **ubĭ**
Where? (adverb) = **ubĭ?**
While = **dum**
Who? = **quis?**
Why? = **cūr?**
Wife = **uxor, -ōris, f.**
Wind = **ventus, -ī, m.**
Wisdom = **sapientia, -ae, f.**
With = **cum** + abl.
Without = **sine** + abl.
Woman = **fēmina, -ae, f.**
Wood, forest = **silva, -ae, f.**
Word = **verbum, -ī, n.**
Work (noun) = **opus, operis, n.**
Work, I = **labōrō, -āre, -āvī, -ātum**
Wound (noun) = **vulnus, vulneris, n.**
Wound, I = **vulnerō, -āre, -āvī, -ātum**
Wretched = **miser, -era, -erum**
Write, I = **scrībō, -ere, scrīpsī, scrīptum**
Year = **annus, -ī, m.**
You (plural) = **vōs**
You (singular) = **tū**
Young man = **iuvenis, iuvenis, m.**
Your (belonging to you (plural)) = **vester, vestra, vestrum**
Your (belonging to you (singular)) = **tuus, -a, -um**